laurie polich-short

STUDIES ON THE GO

ROMANS

Z **ZONDERVAN**®

ZONDERVAN.com/
AUTHORTRACKER
follow your favorite authors

youth
specialties

YOUTH SPECIALTIES

Studies on the Go: Romans
Copyright 2009 by Laurie Polich-Short

Youth Specialties resources, 1890 Cordell Ct. Ste. 105, El Cajon, CA 92020 are published by Zondervan, 5300 Patterson Ave. SE, Grand Rapids, MI 49530.

ISBN 978-0-310-66874-9

Cover design by Toolbox Studios
Interior design by SharpSeven Design

Printed in the United States of America

13 14 15 16 /DCI/ 22 21 20 19 18 17 16 15 14 13 12 11 10 9 8 7 6 5

DEDICATION

To Jerome Drew Short—God's redemptive gift in my life.

ACKNOWLEDGMENTS

Jon Ireland, Jono Shaffer, Alan Anderson, Uriah Venegas: What an amazing privilege to do ministry with you.

Ryan Warner, Jonny Gaspardis, Teyler Sorenson: Thanks for loving the kids at Ocean Hills—you are the inspiration for this book.

Stacy Sharpe, Melissa Johnston, Vicki Stairs: What would I do without my three best friends?

Tyrone Polich and Judith Polich Coe: Thank you for modeling second chances in your lives and marriages—and for bringing me into this world. I love you!

CONTENTS

INTRO
Studies on the Go: Romans

Are your teens ready to have their lives changed? That's what the book of Romans tends to do. Martin Luther read the book of Romans and started the Reformation. Augustine read the book of Romans and became known as "Saint Augustine." Karl Barth read the book of Romans and influenced some of the world's greatest Christians. What will the book of Romans do to you?

With *Studies on the Go: Romans*, you'll be armed with all the questions you need to lead 30 studies through Paul's letter to the church in Rome. Your students will begin to grasp the life-changing truths of this great book and have a better understanding of how these truths can shape their lives. Admittedly, this is a tough book—it deals with many complex (and often controversial) theological issues. But it's also a rich book. And my guess is you'll wrestle with these questions just as much as your kids will.

Questions have the power to change people. That's what makes them so important. You'll notice three kinds of questions in these studies—Observation, Interpretation, and Application. Observation questions take your teens *to* the text, Interpretation questions lead them *through* the text, and Application questions help them *live* the text. Each study is prefaced by a short introduction that gives shape and form and context to the study. The sessions begin with sharing questions (designed to break the ice) and end with group exercises (designed to bring the lesson home). There are also reproducible Quiet Time Reflection sheets after the studies for those who want to dig deeper into the Bible on their own.

Remember: Do the parts of this book that suit your group best; you don't have to use every question in the book, and you can feel free to add to them or alter them.

That's a brief tour of *Studies on the Go: Romans*. Enjoy this ministry tool, and remember—your Savior did some of his finest work through his questions. Perhaps you will, too!

1. WILL YOU TAKE THE CALL?
Romans 1:1-17

OVERVIEW

In the "olden" days, before cell phones, people used to make collect calls—and the experience could leave you hanging. The operator would announce your name to the person who answered the call and ask whether he or she would accept the charges. The person had to accept the charges for your call to go through. That person's response dictated the outcome of the call.

Paul's call to become a Christ-follower was a little like a collect call—at some point he had to decide whether or not he would accept the charges. When Paul refers to himself as a "servant of Christ Jesus" (v. 1), we clearly see how Paul answered his call.

This opening passage of Romans reveals that Paul isn't the only one who received God's call; God extends that same call to you and me (vv. 5-6). And there's only one way to pay the charges—by giving God your life.

SHARE
Warm-Up Qs (use one or more as needed depending on your group)

- Who calls you most frequently? Who do you wish would call you more often?

- What causes you to determine whether or not to take a call? Is there anyone you take calls from no matter what you're doing or how busy you are?

- Have you ever felt "called" to do something (i.e., led by God)? If so, what?

OBSERVE
Observation Qs

- How does Paul describe himself in v.1? What was he called to be? What was he "set apart" for?

- Who is Paul writing to? (v. 7) What are the first things he says to them? (vv. 7-8)

- Why does Paul want to see the Romans? (vv. 11-12) What does he want to happen when/if they see each other? (v. 12)

- According to Paul in vv. 16-17, what kind of righteousness does the gospel provide? Does it have to do with us—or God?

THINK
Interpretation Qs

- What do you suppose it means to be "set apart for the gospel of God"? (v. 1) Do you believe this applies only to Paul—or to all Christians?

- In v. 5, Paul says he's calling people to the "obedience that comes from faith." What do you think that means? Is it possible to have faith without obedience? Why/why not?

- What does Paul reveal about his relationship with God in vv. 8-13? What does he reveal about his relationship with the Romans?

- Why do you suppose Paul makes a point to say he's not ashamed of the gospel? (v. 16) Do you believe he had a reason for saying that? Why might Christians be ashamed of the gospel?

APPLY

Application Qs

- How consistently do you show your faith in God through your obedience? All the time, sometimes, or none of the time?

- Is there an area of your life where you need to obey God more? What would that require you to do?

- Paul shows in this passage that he lives his life totally directed by God. Do you feel God directs you in your decisions and actions?

- If part of our calling is to share our faith with others, with whom do you believe God wants you to share your faith? How can the group pray for you?

OPTIONAL ACTIVITY

As a group, read the little pamphlet called *My Heart, Christ's Home* by Robert Boyd Munger (InterVarsity Press). Then go around the group and have your teens share which room they have the hardest time letting Christ into, and what changes they'd need to make for Christ to be more welcome there.

QUIET TIME REFLECTIONS

Day 1: Romans 1:1-4

1. What word or verse stands out to you from this passage? Why?

2. What does Paul call himself in v. 1? Do you think of yourself this way?

3. Spend time thinking today about what it means to be "set apart" for God.

Day 2: Romans 1:5-6

1. What word or verse stands out to you from this passage? Why?

2. In v. 6, to whom does Paul say God's call is extended? Do you believe you're included in this?

3. Spend time today thinking about your call—and whether or not you're living it out.

Day 3: Romans 1:7-10

1. What word or verse stands out to you from this passage? Why?

2. How does Paul say he remembers his friends in Rome? (vv. 9-10) How often do you pray for your friends?

3. Spend time remembering your friends in prayer—and think about ways to encourage them.

Day 4: Romans 1:11-13

1. What word or verse stands out to you from this passage? Why?

2. What does Paul want to give his friends in Rome? (v. 12) Do you feel this way?

 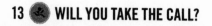

3. Spend time today thinking about how you and your Christian friends can encourage each other in your faith.

Day 5: Romans 1:14-15

1. What word or verse stands out to you from this passage? Why?

2. To whom is Paul obligated to preach the gospel? (v. 14) Does this include everyone?

3. Spend time today thinking about whether or not you're sharing the gospel with others. Is there anyone in particular whom God may want you to share it with?

Day 6: Romans 1:16-17

1. What word or phrase stands out to you from this passage? Why?

2. Why does Paul say he's not ashamed of the gospel? Do you feel the same way?

3. Spend time reflecting if fear or shame has kept you from sharing your faith. After reading these verses, why should you feel confident about your faith?

Day 7: Romans 1:1-17

Read through the whole passage and write out the verse that spoke to you the most this week. Meditate on that verse today—and for an extra challenge, memorize it!

2. THE FROG IN THE KETTLE
Romans 1:18-32

OVERVIEW

Have you heard that if you put a frog in cold water and slowly heat the water to a boil, the frog won't jump out? That the frog will just sit there and boil to death? Well, the truth is that it's an urban legend (the frog will exit the water when it gets too hot). But that doesn't mean it's not a fitting analogy for how we all fall into sin.

Sin usually takes root when we want to do something we know God doesn't want us to do. After enough rationalizing, we finally do it—and then we feel bad, promising never to do it again. But once the sin has been tried, the temptation to repeat it increases—and we find it harder to stay away. So we stay in the pot when we should jump out.

If you look over the list of sins Paul describes in this passage, they probably seem so extreme that you don't believe you'd ever commit them. But that's not how sin usually works. A little sin lures you into a pot of cold water, and it increases to a big sin, slowly boiling you to death.

This session will help your teens see that no matter how warm and cozy sin feels at first, it eventually leads to death. And God's desire is to give you life.

SHARE
Warm-Up Qs

- Do you believe we're born with a sense of right and wrong, or do we learn it?

- Who/what has the greatest influence on the way you live your life? In what way have you been influenced by these "forces"?

- Think about the last time you did something you knew was wrong. Were there any decisions you made beforehand that contributed to your action(s)?

OBSERVE
Observation Qs

- Look at vv. 18-19. Who/what is the wrath of God against? What is the reason?

- According to v. 20, what part of God has been clearly seen by everyone in the world?

- What did people exchange God's glory for? (v. 23) According to v. 25, what was the result?

- How is the progression of sin described in vv. 28-32? How does it start? (v. 28) How does it end? (v. 32)

THINK
Interpretation Qs

- Why do you believe God is angered by sin? Is it because God loves us—or wants to restrict us?

- After reading this passage, do you suppose God has a different standard for nonbelievers as opposed to believers? Why/why not?

- What do you suppose Paul means when he writes, "God gave them over to shameful lusts"? (v. 26) Do you believe our choice to sin one time makes it easier to sin again? Why/why not?

- Do you believe all sin is a choice? Why/why not? According to v. 28, how does our mind make a difference in what we choose to do?

APPLY
Application Qs

- Do you believe all the sins mentioned in this passage are relevant to us today? Is there anything that used to be a sin that our culture views differently now? Do you believe God's standards change with our culture?

- Of all the sins listed in vv. 26-31, which are the hardest for you to avoid?

- What impact do your thoughts/circumstances have on whether or not you choose to sin? When (or where) do you find yourself tempted most?

- What helps you "retain the knowledge of God" (v. 28)—being around Christians? Regular Bible reading? Prayer? Is there anything you need to work on in your effort to stay close to God?

OPTIONAL ACTIVITY

If you're able, do an object lesson by putting a frog in a pot of hot water, and watch it jump out. Then explain the urban legend that if you put the frog in cold water and slowly heat it to a boil, the frog would stay in and die. (Please DON'T try to disprove the myth as part of the object lesson!) Use it as a springboard for discussion about the progression of sin...that we're more likely to fall into sin if we progress into it little by little, decision by decision. Your teens can/will make decisions about friends, parties, relationships that will impact how strong their resolve will be.

QUIET TIME REFLECTIONS

Day 1: Romans 1:18-20

1. What word or verse stands out to you from this passage? Why?

2. According to these verses, what shows us that God exists? What evidence do you see that God exists?

3. Spend time today observing all the ways you can see God in the world around you.

Day 2: Romans 1:21-23

1. What word or verse stands out to you from this passage? Why?

2. For what did people exchange the glory of God? Can you think of some idols people worship today in place of God?

3. Spend time thinking today about any "idols" you may worship in place of God, and reaffirm your commitment to the one, true God.

Day 3: Romans 1:24-25

1. What word or verse stands out to you from this passage? Why?

2. Do you believe these verses hold true in our world today? Where have you seen examples of this?

3. Spend time today thinking about how you can keep God first in your life.

Day 4: Romans 1:26-27

1. What word or verse stands out to you from this passage? Why?

2. How do you see Paul's words as being true in today's culture?

3. Spend time today praying for those you know who struggle with gay or lesbian lifestyles. Pray for a heart of compassion and understanding for them. (And if you're struggling with these issues, don't struggle alone—talk to your youth pastor or another trusted adult.)

Day 5: Romans 1:28-31

1. What word or phrase stands out to you from these verses? Why?

2. Which of these attitudes or sins have you struggled with? Are there any you are struggling with now?

3. Spend time praying for forgiveness and for your heart to be clean—with God and others.

Day 6: Romans 1:32

1. What word or phrase stands out to you from this verse? Why?

2. There are two things in this verse that Paul says are wrong. What are they? What do you think it means to "approve of those who practice [these things]"?

3. Spend time today thinking how you can love people without approving of their sinful actions.

Day 7: Romans 1:18-32

Read through the whole passage and write out the verse that spoke to you the most this week. Meditate on that verse today—and for an extra challenge, memorize it!

3. KNOWING RIGHT FROM WRONG
Romans 2:1-16

OVERVIEW

Have you ever noticed how much easier it is to point to other's mistakes than to admit our own? It's almost as if we see other people's faults through a magnifying glass. In this passage Paul takes that magnifying glass and turns it into a mirror. And he invites us to take a closer look at ourselves.

One of the hardest things about becoming a Christian is admitting that we're sinners. Somehow the word *sinner* seems so degrading that we feel as though we can't be *that* bad. But when we look at the list of sins in this passage, we see that being judgmental and unrepentant are at the top of the list. Suddenly we realize that no matter how many sins we've managed to avoid, there are at least an equal number of sins we've managed to commit.

Admitting our problem is half the solution, because then we know we need help. And that's what Paul is getting at in this passage.

Our consciences may help us see what's wrong—but Paul shows us we need something bigger than our consciences to help us move toward what's right.

SHARE
Warm-Up Qs

- Have you ever experienced a "guilty conscience"? (In other words, times when your conscience wasn't clear; when you felt guilty about something.) If so, what did it feel like?

- In what ways is your conscience similar to God's voice? Do you believe they're one and the same?

- Do you tend to be more judgmental toward others—or yourself? On a scale of 1-10 (1=nonjudgmental; 10=highly judgmental), how judgmental are you—to yourself and also to others?

OBSERVE
Observation Qs

- What warning does Paul give about judging others? (v. 1) According to this verse, what happens to us when we judge?

- What do vv. 6-8 say about how God will judge us? What brings God's wrath and anger according to v. 8?

- Look at vv. 9-10. Who's eligible to receive God's glory, honor, and peace? Is anyone excluded?

- According to v. 12, what happens to people who sin apart from the Law? What happens to people who are under the Law?

THINK
Interpretation Qs

- Why do you suppose v. 1 says we're condemning ourselves when we judge others?

- In v. 4 Paul says God's kindness, not God's judgment, leads us toward repentance. What do you suppose this means? Do you believe people are more motivated by God's love or God's judgment?

- Look at vv. 8-9. What do you suppose it means to "reject the truth and follow evil"? Which is harder—following God or following evil? Why?

- Look at vv. 14-15. Do you believe we need to know the Law to understand what's right and wrong? Or do we know because of our consciences?

APPLY
Application Qs

- Have you ever judged someone else to make yourself feel better? If so, did it work?

- Have you ever felt judged by someone else? Without naming names, how did it make you feel?

- Do you feel more peace when you're following your conscience? If so, how do you know your conscience is telling you what to do (as opposed to other influences)?

- Would you describe yourself as someone who listens to God's voice? Is there anything God might be prompting you to do (or not do) in your life right now?

OPTIONAL ACTIVITY

Choose three of your group members and blindfold one of them. Have the other two lead the blindfolded member around the room—one giving correct directions, the other giving wrong directions. (Caution: Make certain the teen giving incorrect directions doesn't lead the blindfolded one into any danger or hazards.) See how long it takes for the blindfolded teen to listen only to the member giving good directions. Debrief by comparing this experience to God's voice inside us—and whether we listen to it or not.

QUIET TIME REFLECTIONS

Day 1: Romans 2:1-4

1. What word or phrase stands out to you from these verses? Why?

2. Have you ever passed judgment on someone else without considering your own actions? How do these verses speak to you?

3. Spend time today thinking about how you can be more of a person of grace than judgment.

Day 2: Romans 2:5-6

1. What word or phrase stands out to you from these verses? Why?

2. What are we doing when we're stubborn and unrepentant and refuse to forgive others? According to these verses, how will God respond to these actions?

3. Spend time today thinking about the areas where you're stubborn and unrepentant, and how you can let God break through and change you.

Day 3: Romans 2:7-8

1. What word or phrase stands out to you from these verses? Why?

2. What should we seek according to these verses? Do you seek these things in your life?

3. Spend time today thinking about how you can be the kind of person described in v. 7.

Day 4: Romans 2:9-11

1. What word or phrase stands out to you from this passage? Why?

2. What are some of the things that lead to trouble and distress? Are there any areas of your life where you reject the truth and follow evil?

3. Spend time confessing those areas of your life where you need God's cleansing and make a commitment to instead seek those things that bring God glory.

Day 5: Romans 2:12-13

1. What word or phrase stands out to you from these verses? Why?

2. Where does righteousness come from—knowing the Law or obeying it? Where in your life are you having trouble obeying God?

3. Spend time thinking of those areas of your life where you need to obey God. (Remember that God is always willing to forgive and offer you a new start!)

Day 6: Romans 2:14-16

1. What word or phrase stands out to you from these verses? Why?

2. What do non-Christians show by unintentionally following God's laws? Do you believe all people have an innate sense of right and wrong? If so, why?

3. Spend time today thinking about how you can respond better to your conscience telling you what's right and wrong, and thank God for the conscience he gave you.

Day 7: Romans 2:1-16

Read through the whole passage and write out the verse that spoke to you the most this week. Meditate on that verse today—and for an extra challenge, memorize it!

4. JEWISH LAW AND CHRISTIAN FAITH
Romans 2:17-29

OVERVIEW

Imagine that you and a friend are sailing. Suddenly your boat capsizes, and you find yourselves dog-paddling in the ocean. Your friend turns to you and says, "It's a good thing I know a lot about sailing. We're exactly 500 miles from shore in shark-infested waters, and our position is due west." Somehow this information doesn't comfort you in your predicament. You don't need knowledge about how far you are from shore—you need help getting there!

The Jews prided themselves on their knowledge of the Law—they had a corner on God's standards. But knowing God's standards only made their situations worse. God gave them the Law to bring their problem (i.e., sin) into focus. But the Jews needed something bigger than the Law to save them. That's what Paul is getting at in this passage.

The bottom line is, knowing you're 500 miles from shore doesn't bring you any closer to getting there. Start swimming, and you'll find out.

SHARE
Warm-Up Qs

- How do you suppose our society would function if we had no laws? Would you like it better or worse?

- Are there any laws you view as unnecessary? Which laws do you view as the most important?

- If you had to describe the difference between being a Jew and being a Christian, what would you say? Do you think it's possible to be both?

OBSERVE
Observation Qs

- Look at vv. 17-23. Who is Paul questioning in these verses? What does he keep asking them in different ways?

- What does Paul say the Jews are responsible for in v. 24?

- According to v. 25, when does circumcision (or being a Jew) have value?

- How does Paul describe what it means to be a Jew in vv. 28-29?

THINK
Interpretation Qs

- How would you describe Paul's tone (or emotion) in vv. 17-24? Does he seem angry? If so, why do you believe that is?

- What is Paul accusing the Jews of in v. 24? Do you believe Christians who don't live out their faith give God a bad name?

- Why do you suppose Paul says a man is not a Jew if he is only one outwardly? (v. 28) Do you believe that's true about Christians, too?

- Look at Romans 3:1-2. What advantages do you see in the Jews having the Law? What disadvantages do you see?

APPLY
Application Qs

- In what ways does the Law show us our need for God? If you had to obey the Law in order to gain God's favor, would your relationship with God be any different?

- What laws from God do you have the most trouble keeping? (See Exodus 20 if you don't know them.)

- Would you describe yourself as an "outward Christian" or an "inward Christian"—or both? Why?

- What's one thing you need to work on when it comes to living your faith? Do you tend to be more concerned with your heart—or your outward appearance? Why?

OPTIONAL ACTIVITY

Pass out a sheet of paper and a pen to each of your group members. On one side of the paper, have them write down some of the outward signs that show people they're Christians (e.g., getting baptized, going to church, etc.). On the other side, have them write down some of the inward signs (e.g., prayer life, obedience, etc.). Then have them circle all the actions that apply to them. Which side has more actions circled? Use it as a springboard for discussion.

QUIET TIME REFLECTIONS

Day 1: Romans 2:17-21

1. What word or phrase stands out to you from these verses? Why?

2. What is Paul condemning the Jews for? Have you ever judged someone else for something you've done yourself?

3. Spend time today thinking about how you can be a better witness to others through your actions and words.

Day 2: Romans 2:22-24

1. What word or phrase stands out to you from these verses? Why?

2. What do you think it means to blaspheme God's name? Why do you suppose Paul says this to the Jews?

3. Spend time today thinking about how you represent God to the world.

Day 3: Romans 2:25

1. What word or phrase stands out to you from this verse? Why?

2. According to Paul, when does circumcision have value? Why is it important that religious signs (such as baptism or circumcision) are matched by our behavior?

3. Spend time today evaluating if others would know you're a Christian based on your behavior.

Day 4: Romans 2:26-27

1. What word or phrase stands out to you from these verses? Why?

2. According to Paul, which is more important: Outward religious signs or how we live our lives? Which is more important to you?

3. Spend time today thinking about non-Christians you may know who live more as Christ commands than you do. In light of this, what about your life needs to change?

Day 5: Romans 2:28

1. What word or phrase stands out to you from this verse? Why?

2. According to this verse, can someone be a Jew only outwardly? Do you think the same thing is true for Christians?

3. Spend time today thinking if you have ever been merely an "outward Christian."

Day 6: Romans 2:29

1. What word or phrase stands out to you from this verse? Why?

2. What's the difference between being a Jew outwardly and being a Jew inwardly? In the same way, what's the difference between being a Christian outwardly and being a Christian inwardly? Where should Christians be focused on getting their praise?

3. Spend time today thinking whether you're more concerned with what others think—or about what God thinks.

Day 7: Romans 2:17-29

Read through the whole passage and write out the verse that spoke to you the most this week. Meditate on that verse today—and for an extra challenge, memorize it!

From *Studies on the Go: Romans* by Laurie Polich. Permission to reproduce this page granted only for use in buyer's youth group. Copyright © 2010 by Youth Specialties. www.youthspecialties.com

5. NO ONE IS GOOD
Romans 3:1-31

OVERVIEW

When was the last time you read "Humpty Dumpty"? It's not a happy story. It's a sad story, told in a happy sort of way. And that's a little of the tactic Paul uses in this chapter.

Paul is continuing to deliver some bad news, but he uses poetry and Scripture to do it. Normally when people write verses to one another, they quote their favorite verses. Paul communicates his message by quoting some "un-favorite" verses, and this makes his point even more profound.

In this chapter Paul makes it clear that we are all sinners—Jews and Gentiles alike. No one can stand blameless before God. The verses Paul uses are grim and despairing, and the Jews can't argue with him because he quotes right from their Scriptures. But the verses don't speak only to the Jews—they contain bad news for us all.

We're fallen people, and we need more than "the king's horses and the king's men" to put us back together again.

What we need is the King.

SHARE
Warm-Up Qs

- Would you describe yourself as a good person? Why/why not?

- What indications do you see in the world that all people are capable of evil?

- If someone said to you, "All good people go to heaven," how would you respond?

OBSERVE
Observation Qs

- According to v. 9, who is more righteous—Jews or Gentiles? Who does Paul say is righteous in vv. 10-12?

- According to v. 20, what is the purpose of the Law?

- Look at vv. 21-23. Where does our righteousness come from? What does v. 22 say makes us righteous before God?

- What part does Jesus play in our righteousness? (vv. 24-25) According to v. 27, why is all boasting excluded?

THINK
Interpretation Qs

- If the Law cannot make us righteous, why do you think it exists?

- Do you think everyone is "alike" in their sin? Or are some people worse than others? How do you interpret vv. 22-23?

- Why do you believe it was necessary for Christ to die? (v. 25) What does this tell you about God? What does this tell you about us?

- Since we're justified by faith, do you believe it matters how we live? (See v. 31.) If so, why?

APPLY
Application Qs

- Do you ever feel God working in you to steer you away from evil? How much do you allow this power to work in your life?

- Knowing God's righteousness is a gift—and there's nothing you can do to earn it—are you motivated to live better or worse?

- Would you say your faith is more dependent on God—or yourself? Why?

- If our righteousness is from God, what do you suppose it means to live a righteous life? In what areas do you need to depend more on God?

OPTIONAL ACTIVITY

"Report Cards." Pass out large index cards to your group and have everyone write their names at the top of their cards. Have everyone give themselves grades based on how good they think they are. Then have them give themselves grades based on how others see them. Have them share their grades, and why they gave themselves those grades.

QUIET TIME REFLECTIONS

Day 1: Romans 3:1-4

1. What word or phrase stands out to you from these verses? Why?

2. According to these verses, what's the advantage of being a Jew? In what way do the Jews have a special relationship with God?

3. Spend time today thinking about any Jewish people you know, and what you can learn from their faith.

Day 2: Romans 3:5-8

1. What word or phrase stands out to you from these verses? Why?

2. What is Paul saying in these verses? Why is it important that we don't use God's grace as an excuse to sin?

3. Spend time today thinking about how you can love God through your obedience.

Day 3: Romans 3:9-20

1. What word or phrase stands out to you from these verses? Why?

2. According to these verses, who can be declared righteous? What, then, is the role of the Law if none of us can keep it?

3. Spend time today thinking about why you need God's grace in your life.

Day 4: Romans 3:21-24

1. What word or phrase stands out to you from these verses? Why?

2. Where does our righteousness come from? Is it through our actions or our faith? Is this true for everyone?

 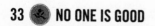

3. Spend time today thinking about whether you really believe your righteousness is from Jesus alone—and if you don't, talk to your youth leader about it.

Day 5: Romans 3:25-27

1. What word or phrase stands out to you from these verses? Why?

2. How did Jesus become our righteousness? Why do we have no reason to boast?

3. Spend time today thinking about the sacrifice Jesus went through to give you righteousness.

Day 6: Romans 3:28-31

1. What word or phrase stands out to you from these verses? Why?

2. According to these verses, does faith wipe out (or *nullify*) the Law? If not, what value does the Law still have?

3. Spend time today thinking about how our faith can be seen in the way we uphold the Law.

Day 7: Romans 3:1-31

Read through the whole chapter and write out the verse that spoke to you the most this week. Meditate on that verse today—and for an extra challenge, memorize it!

6. RIGHTEOUSNESS BY FAITH
Romans 4:1-25

OVERVIEW

Have you ever received credit for something you didn't do? At first you're tempted not to say anything. However, it gets a little awkward if someone goes on and on about what "you" did.

Imagine for a minute if the person who actually did it was standing right beside you—and didn't say a word. She just let you get the credit for what she did. Would you feel better—or worse?

In this chapter Paul continues to drive home the point that we're not justified by works but by faith in the One who did the work for us. This was obviously hard for the Jews to accept, since they spent their whole lives working for justification. So Paul uses their patriarch Abraham to illustrate his point.

Abraham's belief in God, rather than his works "for" God, made him righteous. And Paul tells his story of faith to prove this point. Your teens will see in this session that Abraham's greatest task was to believe. And that's the same task that faces us all.

SHARE
Warm-Up Qs

- Have you ever received credit for something you didn't do? If so, how did it feel?

- Have you ever observed others getting credit for things they didn't do? How did that feel?

- Do you believe people should be punished for the things they've done wrong—or should they be forgiven with no punishment?

OBSERVE
Observation Qs

- According to v. 3, what did Abraham receive credit for?

- Who is "blessed" according to vv. 7-8? Is this just for Jews (the circumcised) or Gentiles (the uncircumcised) or both?

- What promise did Abraham receive in v. 13? What is required to receive this promise? (v. 16) Who is the promise guaranteed to?

- According to vv. 18-21, how did Abraham exercise his faith? What was the result? (v. 22)

THINK
Interpretation Qs

- Why do you suppose Paul emphasizes in this chapter that Abraham is blessed for his faith rather than his works?

- What does Paul mean when he writes Abraham "is the father of us all"? (v. 16) In what way is Abraham our father?

- Look at v. 3. What did Abraham do to be called "righteous"? Why did this make him righteous?

- How does Paul say we will be credited with righteousness? (vv. 23-24) Does it have anything to do with our actions? Why/why not?

APPLY
Application Qs

- Have you ever had to "wait in faith" for God like Abraham did? What effect does waiting have on your faith? Has waiting made your faith stronger or weaker?

- Why do you suppose God is so interested in building our faith? Did this chapter give you any insight into why our faith is important to God?

- On a scale of 1-10 (1=no faith; 10=lots of faith), how much faith do you have?

- Is there anything going on in your life for which you need faith?

OPTIONAL ACTIVITY

Take the report cards from last week, turn them over, and have your group members create columns representing different aspects of their lives (e.g., home life, social life, school life, thought life, etc.). Have them grade themselves in each of these areas, according to how they believe God would grade them. Then have them write across their report cards "believed God, and it was credited to him [or her] as righteousness" (Romans 4:3). Invite your teens to keep these report cards as a reminder that the only "credit" we receive is for our faith.

QUIET TIME REFLECTIONS

Day 1: Romans 4:1-3

1. What word or phrase stands out to you from these verses? Why?

2. What was credited as righteousness to Abraham? How does Paul use this as an argument for the fact that we're made righteous by faith?

3. Spend time today thinking about how much righteousness you'd be credited for because of your faith.

Day 2: Romans 4:4-9

1. What word or phrase stands out to you from these verses? Why?

2. How does Paul describe our righteousness as a gift from God? Why does that make the blessing greater?

3. Spend time today thinking about how we're given righteousness as a gift rather than an obligation.

Day 3: Romans 4:10-15

1. What word or phrase stands out to you from these verses? Why?

2. How does Paul prove that Abraham received his promise by faith rather than the Law? Why do you suppose this is significant?

3. Spend time today thinking about how God's plan has always been for us to gain our righteousness by faith rather than the Law.

Day 4: Romans 4:16-17

1. What word or phrase stands out to you from these verses? Why?

2. Who is Abraham the father of? Do you consider yourself Abraham's offspring?

3. Spend time today thinking about how Abraham is the father of Jews and Christians because he received God's blessing by faith.

Day 5: Romans 4:18-21

1. What word or phrase stands out to you from these verses? Why?

2. Why do you suppose God waited so long to give Abraham his son, Isaac? Do you believe he had a purpose in that?

3. Spend time today thinking how God can use your circumstances to build your faith.

Day 6: Romans 4:22-25

1. What word or phrase stands out to you from these verses? Why?

2. How are we credited with righteousness? Do we have to do anything?

3. Spend time today thinking about how your faith and belief is more important to God than trying to work your way to get to God.

Day 7: Romans 4:1-25

Read through the whole chapter and write out the verse that spoke to you the most this week. Meditate on that verse today—and for an extra challenge, memorize it!

7. HIS LIFE FOR OURS
Romans 5:1-11

OVERVIEW:

In World War II, a Catholic priest named Father Maximilian Kolbe was taken to a concentration camp and ordered to strip naked and line up with the Jews for a random selection. Ten Jews were to be taken to a special cell where they'd be given no food or water until they died. The man next to Father Kolbe was selected, and as the man left the line, Father Kolbe heard him say, "My poor wife; my poor children." In that moment, Father Kolbe decided to take his place.

Romans 5:7-8 reads, "For a good man someone might possibly dare to die. But God demonstrates his own love for us in this: While we were still sinners, Christ died for us." The sacrifice of Father Kolbe was beyond what most of us would ever do. But this passage reminds us that the sacrifice of Christ surpassed even that.

We don't ever have to wonder if God understands our suffering. Jesus proved it by going to the cross. We're never more like God than when we endure pain, hardship, ridicule, or sorrow for the sake of Christ.

But pain and suffering are not the end of the story. Three days after Jesus died, we found out why.

SHARE
Warm-Up Qs

- Has someone ever made a significant sacrifice for you? If so, how did it feel? (If you can't think of anyone, consider what your parents have done for you.)

- Is suffering all bad—or can you think of any good that can come from it?

- Does God seem close or far when you're going through times of suffering? Why?

OBSERVE
Observation Qs

- According to vv. 1-2, how do we have peace with God?

- In vv. 3-4, what does Paul say suffering produces?

- How does God demonstrate his love for us, according to v. 8?

- Look at vv. 9-11. How are we "saved," according to v. 10? What are we saved from? What should be our response? (v. 11)

THINK
Interpretation Qs

- Why does Paul say we should rejoice in our sufferings? (v. 3) How is this possible?

- Look at the progression of suffering in vv. 3-4. Do you think you need to go through all four stages to move from suffering to hope? Why/why not?

- Why do you suppose Paul says Christ died "at just the right time"? Would it have made a difference if we'd gotten our act together before Christ died for us? Why/why not?

- Why do you suppose we need to be saved from God's wrath? (v. 9) Does everyone need to be saved—or only people who are really bad? Why?

APPLY
Application Qs

- Have you ever experienced "the hope that comes from suffering"? If so, when?

- Do you feel that you have peace with God? If so, why? If not, why not?

- Is it hard for you to accept that God's grace is unearned? In what ways do you still work for God's approval?

- In what ways can suffering be considered a gift? Are you going through any kind of suffering at this time? How can you begin to practice the truth of v. 3 in your life right now?

OPTIONAL ACTIVITY

Have group members write down on pieces of paper the worst circumstances they've endured (the descriptions should be anonymous). Then have them fold their pieces of paper and put them in a stack in the middle of the room. Have group members take one piece of paper (making sure it isn't theirs) and share how they'd handle these situations if they happened to them. How would they persevere? What could help them draw near to God? If your teens are open enough, have them reclaim their pieces of paper and pray for each other.

QUIET TIME REFLECTIONS

Day 1: Romans 5:1-2

1. What word or phrase stands out to you from these verses? Why?

2. Do you feel as though you have peace with God? According to Paul, what gives us this peace?

3. Spend time today thinking about whether you have peace with God through your relationship with Jesus.

Day 2: Romans 5:3-5

1. What word or phrase stands out to you from these verses? Why?

2. According to these verses, what does suffering produce? Have you ever experienced this in your life?

3. Spend time today thinking about how you can be thankful for your sufferings because of what they are producing in you.

Day 3: Romans 5:6

1. What word or phrase stands out to you from this verse? Why?

2. Why do you think Paul says Christ died "at just the right time"? Why was this important?

3. Spend time today thinking about how Christ died for us while we were powerless against our sin.

Day 4: Romans 5:7-8

1. What word or phrase stands out to you from these verses? Why?

2. What makes Christ's death for us so significant? What sets it apart from others who have died for people they love?

3. Spend time today thinking about the way God reached out to us in love through Jesus.

Day 5: Romans 5:9-10

1. What word or phrase stands out to you from these verses? Why?

2. According to Paul, what is the process of being reconciled and saved? What does Jesus' death and resurrection have to do with this?

3. Spend time today thinking about being "saved" by God. What have you been saved from? What have you been saved for?

Day 6: Romans 5:11

1. What word or phrase stands out to you from this verse? Why?

2. Why does Paul say we should rejoice? Have you rejoiced over this?

3. Spend time thinking about ways you can rejoice in God today.

Day 7: Romans 5:1-11

Read through the whole passage and write out the verse that spoke to you the most this week. Meditate on that verse today—and for an extra challenge, memorize it!

8. THE FIRST AND SECOND MAN
Romans 5:12-21

OVERVIEW

It's hard to imagine the mind of God when Adam was created. When God told him he could eat from any tree except one, it didn't take Adam very long to decide it was the one tree he wanted most. So Adam disobeyed God. And from that decision on, the descendants of Adam have been following his example.

Perhaps God had in mind that people would choose obedience. But the fact is, God gave us a choice. In giving us freedom, God allowed for the possibility that we would choose *not* to obey. And that's exactly what we've done.

In this passage your teens will learn that the first man, Adam, paved the way for disobedience and death. But the Second Man, Jesus, paved the way for obedience and life. Like Adam, Jesus was given a choice in the garden of Gethsemane.

But the Second Man made a better choice.

SHARE
Warm-Up Qs

- Have you ever done something you knew God didn't want you to do? What was the result?

- Do you feel as though your actions always/sometimes/never have an impact on others?

- Are you more apt to follow a friend who leads you to do something bad—or a friend who leads you to do something good? Why?

OBSERVE
Observation Qs

- Look at v. 12. How does Paul say sin and death came into the world?

- What does v. 15 say about God's grace?

- According to v. 18, what was the result of Adam's sin? What was the result of Jesus' act of righteousness?

- What does v. 20 say happens when sin increases? What does grace bring according to v. 21?

THINK
Interpretation Qs

- Look at v. 12. Do you believe Adam is responsible for all our sin? Why/why not?

- In vv. 15-16, Paul explains the difference between Adam's sin and Christ's gift. How were they different in their influence? Which do you think was greater? Why?

- How was Adam's sin different from Christ's grace in how it was passed on to us? (See vv. 15-16.)

- How was it possible for the increase of sin to bring about the increase of grace? (v. 20) What does that tell you about God's grace?

APPLY

Application Qs

- Do you believe that if you were Adam (or Eve) you would have made a different choice and obeyed God? Why/why not?

- Do you believe God sees you as righteous? Why/why not?

- If you were on a judgment stand and asked why you should be allowed to go to heaven, what would you say?

- Is there any sin in your past for which you have trouble accepting God's forgiveness? If so, how does this chapter speak to that?

OPTIONAL ACTIVITY

Get some flash paper (www.magical-tricks.com) and pass it out to your group. Have them each take a size of paper that represents their sin (you can cut small, medium, and big pieces). One by one, take a match and light their papers. (The paper disappears in a really cool effect—but you may want to practice this before your group time and clear the activity with your supervisor.) Use this object lesson to talk about how God's grace covers ALL our sin, no matter how big it is. The bigger our sins, the bigger the flame of grace.

QUIET TIME REFLECTIONS

Day 1: Romans 5:12-13

1. What word or phrase stands out to you from these verses? Why?

2. How did sin come into the world? Do you think it's all Adam's fault that we bear the consequences of sin? Or do we share the responsibility because of all of our sin collectively?

3. Spend time today thinking about your own sin and how we are all responsible for bringing death into the world.

Day 2: Romans 5:14-15

1. What word or phrase stands out to you from these verses? Why?

2. How is the gift that came through Jesus different from the trespass that came through Adam? Which had the bigger impact?

3. Spend time today thanking God that the gift of Christ's grace is bigger than the consequences of our sin.

Day 3: Romans 5:16

1. What word or phrase stands out to you from this verse? Why?

2. What does Paul say the difference is between the judgment and the gift?

3. Spend time today thinking about how God's grace covers all of our sin.

Day 4: Romans 5:17

1. What word or phrase stands out to you from this verse? Why?

2. What happens to those who receive God's gift of righteousness? Do you believe this has happened to you?

3. Spend time today thinking about what it means to "reign in life."

Day 5: Romans 5:18-19

1. What word or phrase stands out to you from these verses? Why?

2. How is the justification of one man similar to the condemnation of one man in the way each of them came to us? What did Christ do to make us righteous?

3. Spend time today thinking about how Christ's obedience impacted our lives.

Day 6: Romans 5:20-21

1. What word or phrase stands out to you from these verses? Why?

2. What happened when sin increased? What does grace bring us?

3. Spend time today thinking about how God's grace increases when we need it most.

Day 7: Romans 5:12-21

Read through the whole passage and write out the verse that spoke to you the most this week. Meditate on that verse today—and for an extra challenge, memorize it!

9. NEW BODY PARTS
Romans 6:1-14

OVERVIEW

Imagine for a moment that you got into a car accident. You were fine, but your car was totaled. What if you went to the mechanic and said, "I know my car needs to be fixed, but please don't replace any of the body parts. I'm used to the old ones; I want to keep them the way they are."

It seems like a ridiculous illustration, but many people live their spiritual lives just like that. When we give our lives to Christ, we become new creations—and we're supposed to trade in our old body parts for new ones.

This can be painful because we're used to our old body parts. But we need new ones to match our new hearts. Our legs have taken us places we no longer want to go. Our eyes have looked at things we no longer want to see. Our brains have been filled with thoughts we no longer want to think.

Until we renew our entire beings, living the Christian life will be like trying to drive a new car with old body parts.

And that's not a smart way to drive. Or live.

SHARE
Warm-Up Qs

- If you could cast away the body part that gives you the most trouble in your relationship with God, what would it be? (Hand? Mouth? Tongue? Foot?)

- What do you think it means to be "alive in Christ"? Would you describe yourself that way?

- If someone asked if you were mastered by sin or mastered by God, how would you respond?

OBSERVE
Observation Qs

- What question does Paul ask in v. 1? How does he answer it?

- What does Paul say about sin in v. 2? What does v. 3 say happens when we're baptized?

- What do vv. 12-13 say are the two choices for how to handle our body parts? Which does Paul recommend?

- According to v. 14, what shouldn't we be mastered by? What reason does Paul give for this?

THINK
Interpretation Qs

- In vv. 1-2, Paul asks a question and then answers it himself. What point do you think he's trying to make?

- What do you believe it means to be united with Christ in his death and resurrection? (vv. 5-6)

- What happens when we let sin reign in our bodies? (v. 12) How does v. 11 help us with this?

- How does v. 13 show us that we have a choice in how we live? Do you believe we can still make bad choices after we start to follow Christ?

APPLY
Application Qs
- What do you suppose it means to offer the parts of your body to righteousness? Have you ever done this? If so, when?

- Which parts of your body are most often offered for righteousness? Which are not?

- Do any of your body parts need to be repaired (or replaced) in order for you to live out your relationship with God?

- Would it be possible for you to let Jesus have all your body parts? Are there any that are hard for you to give him without taking them back?

OPTIONAL ACTIVITY
Have everyone cut out "paper doll" figures that represent themselves (or you can do this beforehand if you want). Then have them each draw crosses on every body part they've allowed Christ to take over. Have them draw targets on those parts they've had trouble giving to Christ (you'll want to have large enough faces on the dolls to show ears, eyes, mouth, etc.). Let your teens reflect on why those parts are "targets" and how this exercise shows them where they're vulnerable to temptation.

QUIET TIME REFLECTIONS

Day 1: Romans 6:1-2

1. What word or phrase stands out to you from these verses? Why?

2. If grace increases with our sin, why shouldn't we sin more to get more grace?

3. Spend time today thinking about what it means to "die to sin."

Day 2: Romans 6:3-4

1. What word or phrase stands out to you from these verses? Why?

2. How are we called to a new life in Christ? What do you think that means?

3. Spend time today thinking about how Christ has given you a new life. How are you different?

Day 3: Romans 6:5-7

1. What word or phrase stands out to you from these verses? Why?

2. What do you think it means that our old self was crucified with Christ? What part of us died?

3. Spend time today thinking about how you've been freed from sin through Christ's death and resurrection.

Day 4: Romans 6:8-10

1. What word or phrase stands out to you from these verses? Why?

2. What should we live for if we have new life in Christ? How is that different from the way we were before?

3. Spend time today thinking about what it means to live for God.

Day 5: Romans 6:11-12

1. What word or phrase stands out to you from these verses? Why?

2. What do you think it means to count yourself dead to sin? How do we do that?

3. Spend time today thinking about letting God, rather than sin, reign in your body.

Day 6: Romans 6:13-14

1. What word or phrase stands out to you from these verses? Why?

2. What does it mean to offer the parts of our body to righteousness? Is that a choice we make—or does it happen automatically?

3. Spend time today thinking about what parts of your body you still offer to sin, and how you can offer them to righteousness instead.

Day 7: Romans 6:1-14

Read through the whole passage and write out the verse that spoke to you the most this week. Meditate on that verse today—and for an extra challenge, memorize it!

10. A NEW OWNER
Romans 6:15-23

OVERVIEW

Many years ago Bob Dylan wrote a hit song called "You Gotta Serve Somebody." The premise of the song is that all of us—Christians and non-Christians alike—serve *someone* or *something* at every moment—whether we're aware of it or not. That's the message Paul gives us in this passage.

You show whom you're serving by the way you spend your time. You show whom you're serving by the way you spend your money. You show whom you're serving by the sacrifices you make. These things help define your master.

Despite what many in our culture say, when you become a Christian, you actually *don't* lose your freedom—you gain it. Ironically people who believe they're free by "doing their own thing" are actually trapped by the very things they're doing! Jesus' way of "mastering" is by setting his followers free.

When you make Jesus your Lord, he'll help you become the person you were meant to be. That's what your teens will learn in this passage.

If you "gotta serve somebody," why not make it him?

SHARE
Warm-Up Qs

- Which of the following brings you the most freedom: Money, power, intelligence, or beauty? Why?

- If someone asked you who or what has control of your life, how would you respond?

- Do you think freedom means doing everything you want to do at every moment? Why/why not?

OBSERVE
Observation Qs

- What question does Paul ask in v. 15? How does he answer it?

- According to v. 16, what determines whether we're slaves to sin or righteousness?

- According to vv. 18-22, what freedom do we experience when we become slaves to righteousness?

- What are the wages of sin? (See v. 23.) What does God give us in Christ?

THINK
Interpretation Qs

- Look at vv. 15-16. If we're under grace, why shouldn't we just go on sinning?

- What do you suppose it means to be a "slave to righteousness"? (v. 18) How would you describe this kind of person?

- In v. 19, Paul says we should offer ourselves to righteousness, which leads to holiness. Do you believe it's possible to be holy? Why/why not?

- What part does Christ play in our eternal lives? (See v. 23.) Do you believe it's possible to have eternal life without Christ?

APPLY
Application Qs

- Have you ever felt the shame Paul talks about (v. 21) over things you have done? Do you feel guilty or free because of your relationship with God?

- What does the manner in which you spend your time and money say about what's important to you? Does it show you serve God—or something else?

- What is your motivation for obeying God? Do you do it to earn God's favor, or because it's the best way to live?

- Would you describe Jesus as your master? If so, how is this reflected in your life?

OPTIONAL ACTIVITY

Write the word *Slavery* on a large piece of cardboard or construction paper. Then have your group share (or write) what words/phrases/images come to mind when they see that word. Then have them brainstorm all the things we can be slaves of—a substance, a habit, a relationship, etc. Is slavery always negative? Or can you imagine slavery that could be positive? If so, what would that look like?

QUIET TIME REFLECTIONS

Day 1: Romans 6:15-16

1. What word or phrase stands out to you from these verses? Why?

2. What shows us who/what we are enslaved to? What are some things in your life that have power over you?

3. Spend time today thinking about if there's an area or areas of your life in which you're a "slave to sin."

Day 2: Romans 6:17-18

1. What word or phrase stands out to you from these verses? Why?

2. According to these verses, what do we have to be thankful for? Do these verses describe you?

3. Spend time today thinking about whether or not you've been set free from sin and are now a slave to righteousness.

Day 3: Romans 6:19

1. What word or phrase stands out to you from this verse? Why?

2. How are we weak in our natural selves? Have you experienced this weakness? Where do you need God's power most?

3. Spend time today thinking about how to let God control more of your life.

Day 4: Romans 6:20-21

1. What word or phrase stands out to you from these verses? Why?

2. What results from the apparent "freedom" of being controlled by righteousness? Is living under the control of sin really freedom?

3. Spend time today thinking about areas of your life where you don't feel free.

Day 5: Romans 6:22

1. What word or phrase stands out to you from this verse? Why?

2. What benefits are ours when we're set free from sin? Have you experienced this freedom?

3. Spend time today thinking about what it means to be free from sin and controlled by God.

Day 6: Romans 6:23

1. What word or phrase stands out to you from this verse? Why?

2. What are the wages of sin? Are you experiencing God's gift of eternal life?

3. Spend time today thinking about the price Jesus paid so we could have eternal life.

Day 7: Romans 6:15-23

Read through the whole passage and write out the verse that spoke to you the most this week. Meditate on that verse today—and for an extra challenge, memorize it!

11. THE LIFELONG STRUGGLE
Romans 7:1-25

OVERVIEW

This might be my favorite passage of Romans. Why? Because it helps me know that I'm not alone. The struggle Paul discusses in these verses is the same struggle I've felt—as long as I've been a Christian. Paul's discussion of his struggle might be comforting to your teens who feel this struggle, too.

The tongue twisters of this passage describe Paul's battle. What he wants to do he cannot do—and he ends up doing the things that he doesn't want to do. I'd normally assume there was something wrong with him—except I find the same experience within myself.

This passage helps to remind us that Christians aren't spiritual supermen and superwomen who float above the struggles of life. Rather they're Spirit-filled people who live in the midst of the struggles of life.

The good news is this battle won't go on forever. And in the meantime, we have Jesus as our hope. Jesus can rescue us because he won the battle. His victory was secured when he went to the cross.

SHARE
Warm-Up Qs

- Would you prefer to get your directions from an electronic device (e.g., a GPS) or from a person who's with you telling you where to go? Why?

- Have you ever felt as though there was a battle going on within you? If so, what did it feel like? How did the battle get resolved?

- When something is "off limits" do you tend to want it more or less? Why?

OBSERVE
Observation Qs

- What does v. 5 say about the Law's effect on us? What does v. 6 say about how we're released from the Law?

- According to v. 7, how do we know what sin is? Does this verse say the Law helps us in our sin—or just makes us more aware of it?

- How does Paul describe the battle within him in vv. 15-19?

- According to vv. 24-25, who rescues Paul from this battle?

THINK
Interpretation Qs

- Look at what Paul says in v. 5. Why do you suppose he says our sinful passions are "aroused by the law"? Do you believe the Law creates a desire to do the wrong thing?

- Look at vv. 7-10. Why does Paul say the Law is incapable of saving us from our sin? Why is having the Law not enough to change our behavior?

- Look at what Paul says in v. 15 and v. 19. What do you believe Paul means by these statements? Do you suppose he felt this way before he was a Christian—or is this a struggle he encountered only after he became a believer in Jesus?

- In vv. 21-25, Paul describes what goes on inside him and why he needs Christ. Do you believe his words relate to all of us—or are they just Paul's experience alone?

APPLY
Application Qs

- Look at Paul's words in v. 15. Can you relate to these words at all? Have you ever experienced the struggle he is talking about here?

- Do you believe the struggle Paul is talking about in this chapter is felt more before or after someone becomes a Christian? Why?

- In this passage, Paul talks about two natures (sinful and spiritual) battling for control (vv. 18-23). Which nature is winning inside you right now?

- Is there something in your life that you don't want to do but feel really tempted to do? What are some steps you can take to not fall into temptation?

OPTIONAL ACTIVITY

Have three group members stand. Put one in the middle and have the other two take the arms of the person in the middle and pull them. Chances are, the student in the middle will be pulled toward the stronger "puller." (Warning: Please emphasize that pulling should *not* remove the arm from the socket!) Debrief by saying, "If the person in the middle represents you, and the people on either side represent the sinful and spiritual natures, what will make one side win?" (Answer: The bigger/stronger one will win.) Talk about things we do to "feed" our sinful natures (as well as our spiritual natures) in order to control which nature wins the battle.

QUIET TIME REFLECTIONS

Day 1: Romans 7:1-4

1. What word or phrase stands out to you from these verses? Why?

2. How does Paul use the example of the death of a spouse to help us understand our relationship to the Law? In what way are we released from the Law?

3. Spend time today thinking about how we are under Christ rather than the Law.

Day 2: Romans 7:5-6

1. What word or phrase stands out to you from these verses? Why?

2. What have we been released from in Christ? How does this affect the way we serve? Is it out of obligation or grace?

3. Spend time today thinking about how to serve in the new way— according to the Spirit rather than the Law.

Day 3: Romans 7:7-13

1. What word or phrase stands out to you from these verses? Why?

2. What causes us to realize our desire for sin? Do you find that you want something more when you know it's wrong?

3. Spend time today thinking about how laws can't change our desires—only God can.

Day 4: Romans 7:14-20

1. What word or phrase stands out to you from these verses? Why?

2. Can you relate to the struggle Paul describes in this passage? When was the last time you felt torn between doing the right thing and doing the wrong thing?

3. Spend time today thinking about how we still have to wrestle with our sinful nature, even though God has given us the power to overcome it.

Day 5: Romans 7:21-23

1. What word or phrase stands out to you from these verses? Why?

2. What two forces are fighting against each other inside us? Where do we delight in God's law? What keeps us from following it?

3. Spend time today thinking about the two forces inside you, and how to give more power to the force of God in your life.

Day 6: Romans 7:24-25

1. What word or phrase stands out to you from these verses? Why?

2. Who ultimately rescues us from our sinful desires? Why is it important to give more power to our minds than our bodies?

3. Spend time today thinking about how to let your mind have more control over your body.

Day 7: Romans 7:1-25

Read through the whole chapter and write out the verse that spoke to you the most this week. Meditate on that verse today—and for an extra challenge, memorize it!

 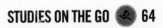

12. CHILDREN OF GOD
Romans 8:1-17

OVERVIEW

Have you ever seen a new mother and father with their child? Everything the child does is a monumental event. First smile, first burp, first step, first poop...and out come the cameras, the videotape, the postings on the Web site.

In this passage, Paul says that's what God is like with us. Not that God gets excited every time we go to the bathroom, but God does get excited over every spiritual victory we achieve. Paul reminds us that we are God's children—and because of that, we are loved. And this passage shows how God comes alongside to help us as we grow in our faith.

Paul writes that we even get to call God "Abba," which is the Aramaic word for "Daddy." With that kind of familiarity we know God is more than a being who distantly cares for us. Rather, God's the daddy who's there for us, loves us, and cares for us in our time of need.

And one day, because we're God's children, we'll get God's inheritance. That's the best part of all.

SHARE
Warm-Up Qs

- When you hear the phrase "Like father, like son" or "Like mother, like daughter," do you resonate with it? In what way(s) are you like your parents?

- Do you suppose people generally grow up to be just like their parents? What would cause them not to do that?

- When you consider God as your father (or parent), is that a positive or negative image for you? Why?

OBSERVE
Observation Qs

- According to vv. 1-3, what did God do to remove our condemnation from sin? What part did Christ play in taking our condemnation away?

- What do vv. 5-8 say about the minds of those who live according to the sinful nature? Who lives according to the Spirit?

- According to v. 9, what are we *not* controlled by if we have the Spirit of God in us? What does v. 11 say will happen to those who have the Spirit of God living inside them?

- What does v. 13 say about the kind of spirit we received from God? What does v. 14 say our relationship with God is?

THINK
Interpretation Qs

- In your own words, summarize what you believe vv. 1-3 say about what God did for us. Why are we no longer condemned?

- What do vv. 5-8 say about how the power of our minds affects how we choose to live? Do you believe that our minds (and what we think about) always control our behavior? Why/why not?

- What do you believe it means to "have the Spirit of Christ"? (vv. 9-10) If you have the Spirit of Christ, do you always follow the Spirit of Christ? Why/why not?

- According to v. 13, what are we supposed to "put to death" in order to experience life? How is this possible?

APPLY
Application Qs

- Would you say that what you think about controls what you do? If so, what do you need to avoid thinking about in order to live more the way God desires?

- Would you describe yourself as having the Spirit of God within you? Would you describe yourself as being controlled by the Spirit of God? Why/why not?

- How does thinking of yourself as God's child deepen your understanding of God's love? Does it make you want to obey God more—or take advantage of God because you know God will always love you?

- Do you notice if other people recognize you as God's child? Is there anything you need to change for others to see more of God in your life?

OPTIONAL ACTIVITY

Have your teens each take a sheet of paper and draw a line across the middle (left to right). Then on the upper half of the page, have them draw line down the middle (top to bottom). This line should not extend to the bottom half of the page.

On the left top corner, have them write *Dad*; on the right top corner, *Mom*. Then on the bottom middle of the paper, have them write *God*. First have them list the traits they think they got from each of their parents (good and bad). Then have them list the traits they've received from God (or the influence of other Christians). Have them circle those traits they believe would cause others to identify them as children of God.

QUIET TIME REFLECTIONS

Day 1: Romans 8:1-2

1. What word or phrase stands out to you from these verses? Why?

2. Why is there no condemnation for those who are in Christ Jesus? Do you experience this in your own life?

3. Spend time today thinking about the fact that in Christ you're not condemned—because of what Jesus did, not because of what you did.

Day 2: Romans 8:3-4

1. What word or phrase stands out to you from these verses? Why?

2. In what way was Christ our "sin offering"? How does that make you feel?

3. Spend time today thanking God for sacrificing his Son on your behalf.

Day 3: Romans 8:5-8

1. What word or phrase stands out to you from these verses? Why?

2. How does the mind control external behavior? What do you believe it means to have your mind set on what the Spirit desires?

3. Spend time today thinking about what you need to do to set your mind on God rather than sin.

Day 4: Romans 8:9-11

1. What word or phrase stands out to you from these verses? Why?

2. What shows that we belong to Christ? In what ways do you feel the presence of God's Spirit in you?

3. Spend time today thinking about the power we have through God's Spirit in us. Are you experiencing this power?

Day 5: Romans 8:12-14

1. What word or phrase stands out to you from these verses? Why?

2. According to Paul, what is our obligation? Do you believe you're led by the Spirit? Why/why not?

3. Spend time today thinking about what "misdeeds of the body" you need to put to death (stop doing).

Day 6: Romans 8:15-17

1. What word or phrase stands out to you from these verses? Why?

2. What does Paul say we are as God's children? What do you believe it means to share in Christ's sufferings so we can share in his glory?

3. Spend time today thinking about how you can share in Christ's sufferings.

Day 7: Romans 8:1-17

Read through the whole passage and write out the verse that spoke to you the most this week. Meditate on that verse today—and for an extra challenge, memorize it!

From *Studies on the Go: Romans* by Laurie Polich. Permission to reproduce this page granted only for use in buyer's youth group. Copyright © 2010 by Youth Specialties.
www.youthspecialties.com

13. ALL THINGS WORK TOGETHER
Romans 8:18-28

OVERVIEW

When you make chocolate chip cookies for the first time, it's kind of a shock when you realize what goes into them. Taken separately, only three of the nine ingredients taste good—the rest you wouldn't want to put in your mouth. But you need all of these ingredients for your cookies to turn out right. And that's a great analogy for what Paul describes in this passage.

In the previous chapter we discussed the struggles we face in our lives, and how one day our struggles will end. But here Paul gives us a picture of what God is *doing* with our struggles. Taken by themselves our sufferings don't "taste" good; in fact, they're unwanted and seem unnecessary—much like some of the ingredients of a chocolate chip cookie. We wonder why God allows them. But all of the sufferings we endure together will bring forth the glory that will one day be revealed.

At the end of this lesson, your teens will see what it takes to make a chocolate chip cookie. But more importantly, the next time they taste one, they'll have a small picture of how God uses ALL things to bring about good in their lives.

SHARE
Warm-Up Qs

- If someone said to you, "There can't be a God because of all the pain and suffering in the world," how would you respond?

- Have you ever seen anything good come out of suffering? If so, describe it.

- What are some things you can think of that you can only accomplish through pain? Of all the goals you've accomplished, can you think of anything that didn't require some pain?

OBSERVE
Observation Qs

- What does Paul say about our present sufferings in v. 18?

- According to vv. 20-21, what was the purpose of God's creation being subject to frustration? What was God's hope?

- What does v. 26 say helps us in our weakness? What kind of help do we receive?

- According to v. 28, in what things does God work for our good?

THINK
Interpretation Qs

- According to vv. 18-21, what do you suppose is the purpose of our suffering? If we didn't suffer, do you believe we'd look to God more or less?

- Why do you suppose Paul compares our suffering to childbirth in v. 22? What (if anything) does that tell you about the purpose of our suffering?

- In v. 24, Paul says "hope that is seen is no hope at all." Do you believe this is true? What do you believe it says about what hope is?

- How would you explain v. 28 to someone who's experienced great suffering?

APPLY
Application Qs

- Has there been any suffering in your life that God has used for good? If so, how?

- If God works good out of our suffering, does that mean we shouldn't be sad about it? Do you believe it's okay to express anger or frustration to God? Have you ever done that?

- Paul says the Spirit helps us when we pray (v. 26). Have you ever experienced a need for the Spirit's help? How can this verse assist you when you don't know what to pray—or even how to pray?

- Do you believe God uses the painful things we experience to help us relate to and minister to others—or is suffering merely the consequence of our actions? Can you think of something painful that has happened to you that God may want to use to help someone else?

OPTIONAL ACTIVITY

Object Lesson: Blindfold your group members and set out all the ingredients needed to bake chocolate chip cookies in individual small bowls. (Guys, if you need help: Butter, sugar, brown sugar, vanilla, baking soda, salt, raw egg, flour, chocolate chips.) Put one ingredient in front of each group member (or more if your group is smaller). Invite them to take as big bites as they want of their ingredients and describe to the group whether they taste good or bad. (Presumably three will taste good; six won't.) Remove their blindfolds and bring out chocolate chip cookies for everyone to taste. Talk about the analogy that "in all things [good and bad] God works for the good of those who love him" (Romans 8:28).

QUIET TIME REFLECTIONS

Day 1: Romans 8:18-19

1. What word or phrase stands out to you from these verses? Why?

2. According to Paul, how do our present sufferings compare with the glory that will be revealed? How does this change your perspective on your circumstances?

3. Spend time today thinking about any sufferings you have endured, and how God will redeem them someday.

Day 2: Romans 8:20-21

1. What word or phrase stands out to you from these verses? Why?

2. What was God's purpose in allowing us to be in bondage? In what ways have you experienced this bondage in your life?

3. Spend time today thinking about how to live in freedom as a child of God.

Day 3: Romans 8:22-23

1. What word or phrase stands out to you from these verses? Why?

2. Why do you suppose Paul compares our situation to labor in childbirth? How do our struggles with our sinful bodies cause us to "groan"?

3. Spend time today thinking about what it will be like to have a new body as a child of God.

Day 4: Romans 8:24-25

1. What word or phrase stands out to you from these verses? Why?

2. Why does hope have to be unseen in order to satisfy the definition of *hope*? What things do you hope for?

3. Spend time today thinking about your hopes for your future.

Day 5: Romans 8:26-27

1. What word or phrase stands out to you from these verses? Why?

2. How does the Spirit help us pray? Have you ever struggled to find the words to pray?

3. Spend time today letting the Spirit pray for you.

Day 6: Romans 8:28

1. What word or phrase stands out to you from this verse? Why?

2. According to this verse, how is God working through all the circumstances of our lives? Do you trust Paul's proclamation?

3. Spend time today thinking about how God will take all the bad things in your life and work them out for your good.

Day 7: Romans 8:18-28

Read through the whole passage and write out the verse that spoke to you the most this week. Meditate on that verse today—and for an extra challenge, memorize it!

14. MORE THAN CONQUERORS
Romans 8:29-39

OVERVIEW

In the movie *Braveheart*, William Wallace leads his people to fight for a cause bigger than themselves. Some of the most stirring scenes are when Mel Gibson (who plays Wallace) stands before his army, inspiring them to face their enemy with courage and might—even if it means death. And William never sends them into battle alone; he always goes with them.

In this passage Paul says we have a God who does the same thing. In the battles of our lives, Jesus doesn't leave us alone. Whether we face trouble or hardship or persecution or death, Paul says nothing can separate us from Christ. Jesus doesn't cheer for us from the sidelines; he's with us in every difficulty we face.

This stirring passage will show your teens that in every battle they face, they're more than conquerors—even if it means death. Because we're fighting a battle that's much bigger than this life. And our eternal victory has already been secured.

SHARE
Warm-Up Qs

- When do you feel closest to God? When do you feel furthest from God?

- Have you ever felt as though God were "against" you? If so, what do you suppose made you feel that way?

- Do you believe God is with us in our struggles—or does God usually let us handle our struggles on our own?

OBSERVE
Observation Qs

- What does v. 29 say God's plan is for those "called according to his purpose"?

- According to v. 30, what's the process of being glorified? Is it our doing—or God's?

- What does v. 32 say is the reason we know God is "for us"?

- In v. 35, Paul asks a question. How does he answer his own question in vv. 38-39?

THINK
Interpretation Qs

- What do you believe it means that God "predestined [us] to be conformed to the likeness of his Son"? (v. 29) Does that mean we have no choice? Or are we a part of that process?

- What do vv. 31-32 say about God's love for us? Do we have to do anything to earn God's love?

- How does Paul say we should feel about trouble and hardship and persecution? (See vv. 36-37.) Do you believe this is realistic? Why/why not?

- Look at vv. 38-39. How do these verses show that God is with us against our circumstances, rather than in our circumstances against us?

APPLY
Application Qs

- How do you know God is with you if you can't see God? In what ways have you experienced God's presence?

- Have you ever felt separated from God because of something that happened to you? If so, does this passage make you feel differently about what happened to you?

- Have you ever felt God's love when going through something difficult? If so, what made you feel that way?

- Is there a battle you're facing right now that you need God's help with? If so, what steps do you need to take to let God help you in the battle?

OPTIONAL ACTIVITY

Have your group members cut out small shields from cardstock. On one side of the shields have them list all the trials, temptations, and persecutions they're facing right now. On the other side, have them write v. 37. Have them keep the shields as reminders of God's protection and power in the midst of hard times.

QUIET TIME REFLECTIONS

Day 1: Romans 8:29-30

1. What word or phrase stands out to you from these verses? Why?

2. What are we predestined by God to be? How much are you like Jesus?

3. Spend time today thinking about if you're fulfilling your calling to be like Jesus.

Day 2: Romans 8:31-32

1. What word or phrase stands out to you from these verses? Why?

2. How does it make you feel that God is for you? Does that change your relationship with God?

3. Spend time today thinking about the ways God has shown he's for you.

Day 3: Romans 8:33-34

1. What word or phrase stands out to you from these verses? Why?

2. Where is Christ right now? How does Jesus protect us from condemnation?

3. Spend time today thinking about how Christ is interceding for you.

Day 4: Romans 8:35

1. What word or phrase stands out to you from this verse? Why?

2. What's the tone of Paul's question? Do you believe Christ is with us against our circumstances—or in our circumstances against us?

3. Spend time today thinking about the times you've felt separated from God and how the question in this verse applies to your own life.

Day 5: Romans 8:36-37

1. What word or phrase stands out to you from these verses? Why?

2. What does Paul call us in these verses? Do you feel as though Christ gives you the strength to conquer all the bad things that happen to you?

3. Spend time today thinking about how Christ's love helps us overcome our circumstances.

Day 6: Romans 8:38-39

1. What word or phrase stands out to you from these verses? Why?

2. Is there anything in Paul's list of circumstances that has made you feel separated from God? How do these verses speak to that?

3. Spend time today thinking about how NOTHING can separate you from God's love.

Day 7: Romans 8:29-39

Read through the whole passage and write out the verse that spoke to you the most this week. Meditate on that verse today—and for an extra challenge, memorize it!

15. THE UNFAIRNESS OF GRACE
Romans 9:1-21

OVERVIEW

When we first read this passage, we're tempted to question God's fairness. But let me ask you something: Do we *really* want God to be fair?

After all, if we received true fairness from God, we'd all be dead. That's what our sins deserve. Instead God has given us what we don't deserve—an opportunity for life. That's what's unfair!

It's unfair that Jesus had to die an innocent death—with our guilt on his shoulders. It's unfair that Jesus bled on our behalf. It's unfair that we don't have to pay for our own sins because God has done it for us. None of this would've happened if God treated us fairly.

One of the mysteries your teens will explore in this passage is that God knows whether or not we'll choose to accept grace. From a certain perspective, this seems unfair. But if you stop and think about it, if we received what was fair—what we truly deserved—there'd be no grace at all. We'd all be condemned.

So I'll settle for the unfairness of grace. And after giving them the chance to think about it, your teens might, too.

SHARE
Warm-Up Qs

- Would you describe God as "fair"? Why/why not?

- Do you believe it's fair if people are forgiven without punishment for bad things they've done? Would it be fair if *you* were forgiven without punishment for the bad things you've done?

- When you see someone speeding, are you glad when they get pulled over? If you drive, would you feel differently if you got pulled over? Why/why not?

OBSERVE
Observation Qs

- According to vv. 4-5, what do the people of Israel have from God? Does Paul say that being Abraham's descendants makes them Abraham's children? (See v. 7.)

- Who does Paul say are God's children in v. 8? Which child of Abraham was the child of promise? (See vv. 7-9.)

- According to vv. 14-15, is God unjust for knowing who will receive mercy and who won't? What does v. 16 say about God's compassion for us? Is it dependent on our actions—or God's?

- What is Paul's argument in vv. 19-21 regarding God's right to make us the way God wants? What analogy does Paul use?

THINK
Interpretation Qs

- Why does Paul have sorrow in his heart? (vv. 1-4) What do these verses tell you about Paul's concern for his Jewish brothers and sisters?

- What case does Paul make in vv. 6-9 regarding who God's children are? What reasoning does Paul use to come to his conclusion?

- Look at vv. 10-15. What does Paul say about predestination here? Do you believe it's "unfair" that God knows what we're going to do before we do it? Do you agree with Paul's conclusion in vv. 14-15? Why/why not?

- Look at vv. 16-21. Does anything make you uncomfortable with these verses? What do you believe Paul's saying here about God's grace?

APPLY
Application Qs

- Why do you suppose it's important that Isaac was the chosen child and not another child who was born the "natural way"? How does that open the door for non-Jews to be considered God's children?

- Have you ever wondered why some people accept God's mercy and others reject it? What (if anything) does this chapter say about that decision?

- If God already knows how we'll respond to him, do you believe we should still share our faith with others? Why/why not?

- Since God has a plan for who you'll become, are there any steps you need to take to help make that happen? Or, since God already knows what will happen, is it better to do nothing and just wait for God's will to unfold in your life?

OPTIONAL ACTIVITY

Pass out clay or Play-Doh to each person in your group. Have them each mold their clay into a person, and then have them share what their clay figures might say about the way they were created. Ask them the following question: "Do you believe your clay figure has a right to be mad at you for the way it was made?" Have them give reasons for their responses.

QUIET TIME REFLECTIONS

Day 1: Romans 9:1-5

1. What word or phrase stands out to you from these verses? Why?

2. How does Paul show his love for his friends in these verses? Do you feel this way about your friends who don't know Christ?

3. Spend time today praying for your friends who don't know Christ.

Day 2: Romans 9:6-9

1. What word or phrase stands out to you from these verses? Why?

2. Who are God's children? Why is it significant that God's children are descendants of Isaac (Abraham's child of promise) rather than Ishmael (Abraham's natural child)?

3. Spend time today thinking about how it's through faith that we become God's children, not because of who our parents are.

Day 3: Romans 9:10-13

1. What word or phrase stands out to you from these verses? Why?

2. How does the story of Jacob and Esau show that it's not by our works that we're chosen by God? (Genesis 26-27)

3. Spend time today thinking about God's sovereignty—how God knows what we're going to do before we do it!

From *Studies on the Go: Romans* by Laurie Polich. Permission to reproduce this page granted only for use in buyer's youth group. Copyright © 2010 by Youth Specialties. www.youthspecialties.com

Day 4: Romans 9:14-16

1. What word or phrase stands out to you from these verses? Why?

2. How does Paul question God's fairness in these verses? What is his conclusion?

3. Spend time today thinking about the mystery of God's grace, and how it's freely given and freely received.

Day 5: Romans 9:17-18

1. What word or phrase stands out to you from these verses? Why?

2. How does God have power over people? Do you believe that means we don't have a choice?

3. Spend time today thinking about how our will and God's will join together to accomplish God's purposes.

Day 6: Romans 9:19-21

1. What word or phrase stands out to you from these verses? Why?

2. What analogy does Paul use to describe what it's like when we question God? How does this make you feel?

3. Spend time today thinking about what God's purpose might be for your life.

Day 7: Romans 9:1-21

Read through the whole passage and write out the verse that spoke to you the most this week. Meditate on that verse today—and for an extra challenge, memorize it!

16. YOU GOTTA HAVE FAITH
Romans 9:22-33

OVERVIEW

In the 1980s a singer named George Michael wrote a popular song in which he repeats one line over and over: "You gotta have faith, faith, faith.... Yeah, you gotta have faith, faith, faith." Though I'm pretty sure Paul wouldn't have agreed with the other lyrics this guy wrote in his song, this is one line he would have loved. And it's actually a great theme for this passage.

Paul says there's one thing the Jews and Gentiles have in common: They both gotta have faith. This was easier for the Gentiles to accept because they never had any other way to relate to God. But the Jews were used to approaching God through the Law—so Jesus, who ushered in the necessity of faith, was a "stumbling stone" for his own people. The message of faith threw the Israelites off balance, which is why Paul keeps drilling this message into his readers' heads.

If a line in a song gets repeated enough, it's hard to stop singing it. That was George Michael's strategy in the 1980s...and it seems to be Paul's strategy in this passage.

"You gotta have faith."

SHARE
Warm-Up Qs

- If you weren't obliged to obey your parents, would you? Why/why not?

- When you obey God, do you do so because you're afraid of the consequences, or because you believe that God knows what's best for you?

- Which do you suppose is more important to God: Our faith or our actions? Why?

OBSERVE
Observation Qs

- According to v. 24, does God call only Jews or only Gentiles or both?

- Paul quotes the Old Testament in vv. 25-26 to describe what happens to those of us who are called. What does Paul write?

- According to vv. 31-32, how is righteousness attained? Who has attained it?

- Look at v. 33. Where did God lay the stone that causes people to stumble? What happens to the person who trusts in this stone?

THINK
Interpretation Qs

- Notice how Paul begins his thoughts in vv. 22-23. Is he suggesting something God might have done—or do you believe he's saying this is what God did?

- What do the Old Testament passages in vv. 25-26 say about our status with God? Did it change? If so, why?

- How do we pursue righteousness? (vv. 31-32) Is it more about our actions or our beliefs?

- Why is Jesus referred to as a "stumbling stone" in vv. 32-33? Who do you suppose he causes to stumble?

APPLY
Application Qs

- What does it mean to be righteous by faith? Would you describe yourself that way?

- Do you believe our actions matter when it comes to our righteousness before God? Or is it only about our faith?

- Does the fact that you were predestined by God to be here, right now, make you feel hopeful, frustrated, or confused? Why?

- Do you believe you know God's purpose for you? Why did God put you where you are? What do you think God might want you to do?

OPTIONAL ACTIVITY

Have each member of your group complete these sentences:

I believe God put me in this part of the world because _____
_____.

I believe God gave me the family I have so that _____
_____.

I believe God gave me the opportunities I have so that _____
_____.

For me to live a life of faith means _____
_____.

QUIET TIME REFLECTIONS

Day 1: Romans 9:22-24

1. What word or phrase stands out to you from these verses? Why?

2. What possibility does Paul suggest in these verses? Do you believe this is more of a hypothesis, or is he stating fact? What point do you suppose he's trying to make?

3. Spend time today thinking about how big God's mind is, and how God's plan is beyond our comprehension.

Day 2: Romans 9:25-26

1. What word or phrase stands out to you from these verses? Why?

2. What Old Testament book does Paul quote from in these verses? What do these verses say about God's love for us?

3. Spend time today thinking about how God called us to be his people through our faith and God's grace.

Day 3: Romans 9:27

1. What word or phrase stands out to you from this verse? Why?

2. What does this verse from Isaiah say about the Israelites? Why are they not automatically saved because they are Jews?

3. Spend time today thinking about the fact that all people come to God through faith—not because of their nationality.

Day 4: Romans 9:28-29

1. What word or phrase stands out to you from these verses? Why?

2. How do these verses point out the consequences of not embracing a life with God through faith? What do you remember about the story of Sodom and Gomorrah?

3. Spend time today thanking God for his grace and your faith—and pray for that faith to be strengthened.

Day 5: Romans 9:30-32a

1. What word or phrase stands out to you from these verses? Why?

2. What do these verses say about trying to work your way to God? Can we get to God through our actions/good deeds?

3. Spend time today thanking God that there's no way to "earn" God's grace—we only receive it through faith.

Day 6: Romans 9:32b-33

1. What word or phrase stands out to you from these verses? Why?

2. Who do you believe the stone is that Paul refers to? Why is this person called a "stumbling stone"? What does Paul say about the one who trusts in this "stumbling stone"?

3. Spend time today thinking about how much you trust Jesus.

Day 7: Romans 9:22-33

Read through the whole passage and write out the verse that spoke to you the most this week. Meditate on that verse today—and for an extra challenge, memorize it!

17. THE WAY OF SALVATION
Romans 10:1-13

OVERVIEW

When I was a senior in high school, I made a confession of faith. I'd been in church my whole life, but that weekend I learned that sitting in church didn't make me a Christian any more than sitting in a garage made me a car. I had to declare my beliefs and identify myself as a Christ-follower. And that's what Paul makes clear in this passage.

No amount of religious zeal brings us to Christ. All we have to do is believe—and confess that belief in some way before others. This confession can happen in a variety of ways—by standing up and "making a decision for Christ," by being confirmed or baptized, or by walking forward during an altar call. There's no single method for becoming a Christian—but there is only one way to salvation. In this passage, we see that it all comes down to belief in Christ. And our confession is what affirms our belief.

It's hard to say "Jesus is Lord" unless you really believe he is. And this study is a good opportunity for your teens to assess whether they've made that confession for themselves.

SHARE
Warm-Up Qs

- Do you think people need to be saved? If so, why?

- If someone asked you if you were saved, what would you say?

- What (if anything) do we need to do to be saved? Do you think salvation is more God's doing—or our doing?

OBSERVE
Observation Qs

- What is Paul's heart's desire for the Israelites according to v. 1? What does v. 2 say he believes about them?

- According to v. 4, where is righteousness found? How is this different from where the Israelites found righteousness? (v. 3)

- What does v. 9 say is the process of being saved?

- According to v. 12, does it matter if you're a Jew or a Gentile? Who does Paul say can be saved in v. 13?

THINK
Interpretation Qs

- Based on Paul's words in vv. 1-3, do you suppose it was hard for the Israelites to let go of their long-held beliefs about righteousness and embrace what Paul was saying? Why/why not?

- Verse 4 says righteousness is available for all those who believe. Why might this be hard for those who've lived their whole lives trying to obey the Law to please God?

- What's the difference between having a set of laws to obey and inviting Jesus to be our Lord? (vv. 5-9) Which do you believe requires more of us?

- Why do you suppose Paul includes both our heart and our mouth in v. 10? Is it important to God to make some kind of public declaration about our faith? Or is it more for us?

APPLY
Application Qs

- According to vv. 9-10, there are only two things we need to do to respond to God's invitation of salvation. Have you done either or both of these things? If so, can you remember when?

- If you haven't yet done what Paul talks about in v. 9, would you like to? If not, what are some of the barriers you sense in your heart and mind?

- Have you ever confessed your faith to friends or family? Is there someone who doesn't know about your faith whom you may need/want to tell? If so, how could you go about doing that?

- What do you believe people's lives should look like if they are "saved"? Is there any difference in the way you live? If not, should there be?

OPTIONAL ACTIVITY

Two Truths and a Lie: Have each of your group members make three "confessions" about themselves—two that are true, and one that's a lie. But instead of guessing the lie, have the other group members guess which ones are true. Debrief with the following questions: *Was there anything new you learned about each other through your "confessions"? Do you think our confessions reveal more about who we are? Do they affect the way others see us? Why might a confession of faith (v. 9) be important?*

QUIET TIME REFLECTIONS

Day 1: Romans 10:1-2

1. What word or phrase stands out to you from these verses? Why?

2. What is Paul's heart's desire? Has it ever been your heart's desire to see someone come to Christ?

3. Spend time today praying for one person you'd love to see come to know Christ.

Day 2: Romans 10:3-4

1. What word or phrase stands out to you from these verses? Why?

2. What righteousness did the Israelites seek? According to v. 4, where does our righteousness come from?

3. Spend time today thanking God for freely giving righteousness to those who believe in Christ.

Day 3: Romans 10:5

1. What word or phrase stands out to you from this verse? Why?

2. How is righteousness by law described? Would you like to receive righteousness based on what you do/how you perform?

3. Spend time today thinking about how different your relationship with God would be if you had to "earn" your righteousness.

From *Studies on the Go: Romans* by Laurie Polich. Permission to reproduce this page granted only for use in buyer's youth group. Copyright © 2010 by Youth Specialties. www.youthspecialties.com

Day 4: Romans 10:6-8

1. What word or phrase stands out to you from these verses? Why?

2. Where does our guidance come from when we receive righteousness by faith? Has your heart ever guided you regarding the right thing to do?

3. Spend time today thinking about the ways you're led by your heart—and how God speaks to you about what God wants you to do.

Day 5: Romans 10:9-11

1. What word or phrase stands out to you from these verses? Why?

2. According to these verses, what do we do to be saved? Have you experienced a time when you've done this? If so, when and how did it happen? If not, why not now?

3. Spend time today thinking about where you are in your relationship with Christ and recall the time when you affirmed your faith in him.

Day 6: Romans 10:12-13

1. What word or phrase stands out to you from these verses? Why?

2. Is there any difference in the way Jews and Gentiles come to know God? Is this true for all people?

3. Spend time today praying for people who need to know that "everyone who calls on the name of the Lord will be saved."

Day 7: Romans 10:1-13

Read through the whole passage and write out the verse that spoke to you the most this week. Meditate on that verse today—and for an extra challenge, memorize it!

18. CALLED TO PROCLAIM
Romans 10:14-21

OVERVIEW

Some things we should keep to ourselves. But our faith in Christ isn't one of them.

In this passage, Paul says part of the reason we're to confess with our mouths that "Jesus is Lord" is for the salvation of others. Because our witness might be the reason someone else comes to believe.

There are many ways to share your faith. One way is to learn to tell others your "story." You may want to let your teens practice this. Usually our spiritual stories are a way to lead into God's story, because the biggest part of our spiritual stories is sharing how Jesus has impacted our lives. And God might use our stories to connect with someone else's story, because our experiences can sometimes help others make a connection to God.

I heard a speaker say, "Your life might be the only gospel someone hears." So even if your students don't always get the opportunity to share their faith, they can live it out. That may be the most important witness of all.

St. Francis of Assisi said it best: "Preach the gospel at all times. If necessary use words."

SHARE
Warm-Up Qs

- Do you think all Christians are supposed to share their faith with others? Why/why not?

- Have you ever shared your faith with another person? If so, what happened? If not, why not?

- What do you think is the biggest barrier that keeps people from sharing their faith?

OBSERVE
Observation Qs

- What reasons does Paul give in v. 14 for why people may not believe?

- According to v. 17, how does faith come? How is the message heard?

- Does Paul say that Israel didn't hear the message? (v. 18) What Old Testament verse does he quote?

- What does v. 21 say God's approach was with Israel? According to this verse, were they responsive to God?

THINK
Interpretation Qs

- What do you suppose v. 14 is saying to us? What is Paul encouraging Christians to do with his questions?

- Look at v. 15. What do you suppose it means to be "sent"? What is the "good news" he's talking about?

- According to vv. 16-17, does faith have to do with the message being spoken or received? Do you believe that all people hear the message when it's spoken to them? Why/why not?

- Look at what Paul says in v. 19. Why do you suppose God would want to make Israel envious? Do you believe God wants to push Israel away—or bring the Jewish people closer to him? (See v. 21.)

APPLY
Application Qs

- Is there anyone you know who seems closed to hearing the gospel? What is it about this person that makes you answer this way?

- On a scale of 1-10 (1=closed about your faith; 10=open to sharing your faith with others), where are you in terms of sharing your faith? Where would you like to be on the scale?

- Does evangelism (sharing your faith) come naturally to you? Or do you feel awkward and tongue-tied when you try to tell someone what you believe?

- Is there someone in your life with whom God might want you to share your faith? If so, what steps could you take this week to begin this process?

OPTIONAL ACTIVITY

Tag Team Role-Play: Have two group members begin by role-playing a conversation between a believer and a nonbeliever in which the believer tries to work into the conversation the opportunity to share his or her faith. After a few minutes, have two more people take over and begin the conversation where it left off. Rotate until all the group members have had an opportunity to participate. Debrief the exercise by discussing what worked and didn't work about the different approaches. Go over a basic outline for how you would share the gospel (if given the opportunity).

QUIET TIME REFLECTIONS

Day 1: Romans 10:14-15

1. What word or phrase stands out to you from these verses? Why?

2. What questions does Paul ask in these verses? Why do you suppose he's asking them?

3. Spend time today thinking about with whom you could share the good news—and pray that you will take that opportunity!

Day 2: Romans 10:16-17

1. What word or phrase stands out to you from these verses? Why?

2. How does faith come? What do you believe it means to "hear" the message? Is it possible to hear it without *really* hearing it?

3. Spend time today praying for the hearts of people you know to be opened to hearing the message of Christ.

Day 3: Romans 10:18

1. What word or phrase stands out to you from this verse? Why?

2. According to this Scripture reference, should the Israelites have heard the message? Do you know anyone who has heard the message but hasn't really listened?

3. Spend time today thinking of people who need to listen to the message—and pray for them.

Day 4: Romans 10:19

1. What word or phrase stands out to you from this verse? Why?

2. How did God try to make Israel envious? What do you think God's purpose was—to draw them in or cast them out?

3. Spend time today thinking about God's grace—and how God pursues people who don't know him.

Day 5: Romans 10:20

1. What word or phrase stands out to you from this verse? Why?

2. How does this Scripture reference reveal God's grace? Is God dependent on our seeking him—or does God seek us?

3. Spend time today thinking of the ways God has tracked you down and brought you to himself.

Day 6: Romans 10:21

1. What word or phrase stands out to you from this verse? Why?

2. How is God described in this verse? In what way does this show God's heart for people who reject him?

3. Spend time today praying for those who've rejected God, that their hearts would be open to Jesus.

Day 7: Romans 10:14-21

Read through the whole passage and write out the verse that spoke to you the most this week. Meditate on that verse today—and for an extra challenge, memorize it!

19. LOVE'S SECRET STRATEGY
Romans 11:1-24

OVERVIEW

Here's a lesson about love to pass on to your teens.

If you love someone, and he or she doesn't love you back, there's one thing you can do to get that person's attention: Open your heart to someone else. It sounds weird, but something about our human nature causes us to want something more when *someone else* is receiving it.

Of course, there is a slight drawback to this plan. If it works, and the person you originally loved starts loving you back, you'll now have two people to love. And that can be a problem—unless of course, you're God.

In this passage, we learn that God uses this strategy in winning the Jews' love. By offering salvation to the Gentiles, God's love has been widened to include more than just the Jews. But there is room in God's love to include both!

Paul hopes that God's love for the Gentiles (through Jesus) will make the Jews jealous enough to embrace Jesus, too. That appears to be God's strategy. And if the Jews do join the Gentiles in embracing Jesus, God's love is big enough for them all.

SHARE
Warm-Up Qs

- Have you ever been jealous of someone? Without naming names, what was it about that person that made you envious?

- If you were trying to get someone to love you, what would you do to win that person's love?

- Have you ever experienced the feeling of wanting something more because someone else had it? If so, can you describe your experience?

OBSERVE
Observation Qs

- According to vv. 1-2, did God reject the Israelites (God's people)? What account does Paul refer to in the Old Testament to make his case? (vv. 2-5)

- What caused some Israelites to be chosen? According to vv. 5-8, was it something they could work to obtain?

- According to v. 11, why was grace extended to the Gentiles? Was it to reject the Israelites forever? What does Paul hope for in vv. 13-14?

- What analogy does Paul give for what happened to the Jews and Gentiles in vv. 17-20? What is his warning to the "grafted in" branches? (vv. 20-22) What will happen to the "cut off" branches if they stop persisting in unbelief? (vv. 23-24)

THINK
Interpretation Qs

- Look at what Paul says in vv. 5-6 about grace. How do you interpret these verses? Why do you think it's important in his reasoning to the Israelites?

- Look at vv. 11-14. What does Paul say God's strategy is for reaching the Israelites? Do you believe the only reason God extends grace to the Gentiles was to make the Israelites jealous? Or is God trying to draw all people (Jews and Gentiles) to himself?

- How would you explain the analogy of the branches Paul gives in vv. 17-21? Who represents the broken-off branches? Who represents the grafted-in branches? What keeps the branches attached? What causes them to be cut off? Is it possible to be cut off and then grafted in again? If so, how?

- What does Paul say about the Israelites in his analogy in v. 24? Why do you believe it's easier for them to be grafted in when they come to faith? How is the Jews' history with God different from the Gentiles'?

APPLY
Application Qs

- What does God's process with the Jews show you about the way God works? Has God ever worked a similar way in your life (i.e., you realized what you were missing when you were distant from God)?

- Why do you suppose God designed his relationship with us as based on grace instead of works? Does this setup make you want to take advantage of God's kindness? Why/why not?

- Most Jewish people have not accepted Jesus as Messiah (but you may know some who have). How does this passage give you more of an understanding of God's heart for this particular group of people?

- Do you suppose others look at your relationship with God and want it for themselves? Why/why not? Who might God want to reach through you?

OPTIONAL ACTIVITY

Have your group members think of someone they admire. Then have them each make a list of all the things they admire about that person. Finally, have them circle those qualities they believe they could have as well. Now ask the following questions: *What holds you back from having (or becoming) the qualities you circled? Is it an attitude you need to change? A fear you need to get over? A sacrifice you need to make? A risk you need to take?* End the activity with the challenge that maybe those people are in their lives for a reason.

QUIET TIME REFLECTIONS

Day 1: Romans 11:1-6

1. What word or phrase stands out to you from these verses? Why?

2. How has God shown that he hasn't rejected the Israelites? Why do they have to abandon their "works mentality" to come to God?

3. Spend time today praying for any Jewish people you know who don't yet have faith in Christ.

Day 2: Romans 11:7-10

1. What word or phrase stands out to you from these verses? Why?

2. Why do you suppose the Israelites had their hearts hardened so their eyes couldn't see? Why do you suppose it was so hard for them to accept a faith based on grace instead of works?

3. Spend time today thinking of anyone you know who still feels they need to "work their way to God."

Day 3: Romans 11:11-12

1. What word or phrase stands out to you from these verses? Why?

2. According to these verses, was God's purpose for the Israelites to reject Christ forever? How does this give you hope for people who haven't yet accepted Christ?

3. Spend time today praying for someone you've given up on—that his or her heart would be opened to Christ, and that you'd have a new heart for that person, too.

Day 4: Romans 11:13-16

1. What word or phrase stands out to you from these verses? Why?

2. How does Paul hope to draw the Jews to faith in Christ? Are people so envious of your faith that they want it for themselves?

3. Spend time today thinking of the witness you are to others—and whether others would want your faith because of what it brings to your life.

Day 5: Romans 11:17-21

1. What word or phrase stands out to you from these verses? Why?

2. How does God speak to the Gentiles in these verses? Why does Paul say we shouldn't boast in our faith at the expense of others who don't yet believe?

3. Spend time today thanking God for your faith and for the grace to continue holding that opportunity out for others. Our faith isn't meant to be kept to ourselves!

Day 6: Romans 11:22-24

1. What word or phrase stands out to you from these verses? Why?

2. What's the only prerequisite for God to receive people— or "graft" them in? In what way do the Israelites have an advantage in terms of being "grafted" in? How does this apply to people you know who grew up in church?

3. Spend time today praying for people who have a church background but don't yet have a relationship with Christ.

Day 7: Romans 11:1-24

Read through the whole passage and write out the verse that spoke to you the most this week. Meditate on that verse today—and for an extra challenge, memorize it!

20. THE BIG PICTURE
Romans 11:25-36

OVERVIEW

Have you ever seen someone sew a needlepoint picture? From the back, it looks like a mess. You can hardly tell what the image is supposed to be. But when you view it from the other side, it looks perfect. That's similar to the way Paul describes God's plan in this passage.

For the last three chapters, Paul has been talking about the Israelites being cut off and the Gentiles being grafted in. The description is similar to the back of a needlepoint. But now Paul observes the "tapestry" from God's perspective. And Paul is in awe of what he sees.

God allowed the Jews' rejection in order to include the Gentiles in his love. But God also did it to win the Jews back. The "big picture" includes both Jews and Gentiles. All the while God's weaving them together with the thread of his grace.

When Paul gets a glimpse of that tapestry, he can do nothing but praise the Artist. And when we get a glimpse of what God's doing in our lives, we do, too.

SHARE
Warm-Up Qs

- Have you ever had something bad happen that turned out better in the long run? If so, what was it?

- Do you believe God's always in control of what happens—even when it's something bad? If so, why do you suppose God allows bad things to happen?

- Have you ever looked at the back of a needlepoint image? How does it compare with the front? What analogy can you draw from this about life?

OBSERVE
Observation Qs

- According to v. 25, why has Israel experienced a hardening of its heart? What does Paul say God's desire is for all of Israel in v. 26?

- What does v. 28 say is the reason the Israelites are loved? What does v. 29 say about God's gifts and God's call?

- What was the purpose of Israel's disobedience according to vv. 30-31? What is God's purpose for all of our disobedience? (v. 32)

- What does Paul say about God's wisdom in vv. 33-34? According to these verses, can we ever fully understand the mind of God?

THINK
Interpretation Qs

- What is Paul's concern about the Gentiles' attitude in v. 25? Why do you suppose they could feel that way?

- Why do you believe God took away the status of the Israelites as God's only chosen people? What does v. 12 tell you about God's heart?

- Do you believe we need to be aware of our disobedience in order to accept God's grace? (vv. 30-32) Why/why not?

- Why do you suppose Paul ends this chapter the way he does? (vv. 33-36) What is he trying to communicate about God's purposes?

APPLY
Application Qs

- Is there anything you don't understand about what God is doing (or not doing) right now? How could Paul's words in vv. 33-36 help in situations you don't understand?

- When you're disobedient to God, do you have a greater appreciation of God's grace? Or is it hard for you to accept?

- Does anything in your life right now look like a mess? If you stepped back and looked at that mess from a different perspective, would it look the same?

- Where do you need to trust God right now? Is it with something you're struggling with—or something you've been subjected to? What would it look like to turn over that part of your life to God? Can you do that?

OPTIONAL ACTIVITY

Pass out one needle and one spool of thread to each person and give everyone in your group a small sewing project (e.g., sewing a button on fabric, sewing on a patch, etc.). Tell your group members that their job is to make it look as presentable as possible in the time you give them. When they're through, have them show the result to the group. Then have them show the group the back of the fabric. Use this as an object lesson to discuss our lives—that God is creating an image from heaven (i.e., the front) that we can't see from earth (i.e., the back). Let them keep their projects as a reminder of how God is working in their lives.

QUIET TIME REFLECTIONS

Day 1: Romans 11:25

1. What word or phrase stands out to you from this verse? Why?

2. What is the purpose of Israel's "hardening in part"? In what way do you see how big God's heart is in this verse?

3. Spend time today thinking about how God's grace is for everyone—and that God desires all people to receive it.

Day 2: Romans 11:26-27

1. What word or phrase stands out to you from these verses? Why?

2. Who do you suppose "the deliverer" is in this Old Testament reference (Isaiah 59:20-21)? Why do you suppose Paul quotes this Scripture?

3. Spend time today thinking about the fact that Jesus fulfilled prophecies in the Old Testament—and that this is further evidence that Jesus is Messiah.

Day 3: Romans 11:28-29

1. What word or phrase stands out to you from these verses? Why?

2. Why does God love the Israelites in a special way? What was their unique call in the Old Testament?

3. Spend time today thinking about how God revealed himself to the Israelites in the Old Testament—and through Jesus in the New Testament.

Day 4: Romans 11:30-32

1. What word or phrase stands out to you from these verses? Why?

2. What is the reason Paul gives for why both Jews and Gentiles need mercy? Do you believe it's necessary to sense your need for grace before you can receive it?

3. Spend time today thinking about your need for grace—and thank God that it's available to you.

Day 5: Romans 11:33

1. What word or phrase stands out to you from this verse? Why?

2. What does this verse say about God's wisdom? Are there times when you find it hard to understand God? How does this verse help you?

3. Spend time today thinking about how God's understanding far surpasses ours—and for that reason we must trust God.

Day 6: Romans 11:34-36

1. What word or phrase stands out to you from these verses? Why?

2. Why does Paul praise God in these verses? Have you ever praised God for the greatness of his mind and wisdom?

3. Spend time today praising God for the greatness of his mind and wisdom.

Day 7: Romans 11:25-36

Read through the whole passage and write out the verse that spoke to you the most this week. Meditate on that verse today—and for an extra challenge, memorize it!

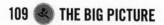

21. LIVING SACRIFICES
Romans 12:1-8

OVERVIEW

When people came together to worship in the Old Testament, they offered sacrifices to express their devotion to God. They carefully selected animals and laid their hands on the animals' heads as a symbol of identifying with the animals before the sacrifice. That's probably what Paul has in mind when he calls us "living sacrifices."

No longer do we offer animal sacrifices because Jesus' death has taken away the need. Instead we offer ourselves as living sacrifices because Jesus' life (and death) has given us the incentive.

So what does it mean to be a "living sacrifice"? Living in a way that honors God. One way to think about it is to consider the difference between what it means to live as a thermostat or a thermometer. A thermometer reflects the temperature in the room; a thermostat *changes* the temperature in the room. As living sacrifices we're supposed to live for God over and above others instead of living for others over and above God.

In this passage, your teens will learn how to use their lives to reflect God's presence and have an impact on the world. That's what it means to be a living sacrifice.

SHARE
Warm-Up Qs

- Would you describe your life as a thermostat (setting the temperature of the room) or a thermometer (going up and down with the temperature of the room)? Why?

- When you hear the word *sacrifice*, what comes to mind?

- What do you believe it means to make our bodies a "living sacrifice" for God? What's one example you can think of regarding how to do that?

OBSERVE
Observation Qs

- According to Paul's words in v. 1, what is our spiritual act of worship? What is our motivation?

- What does v. 2 say about the process of being transformed? What do we need to do? What is the result?

- What image does Paul use in vv. 4-5 to describe our relationships with other Christians? According to these verses, are we alike or different? Do we function separately or together?

- Who has gifts according to v. 6? What kinds of gifts are mentioned in vv. 6-8?

THINK
Interpretation Qs

- Look at Paul's words in v. 1. Why do you suppose he says to "offer your bodies" as an act of worship? How would you define *worship*?

- Why do you believe we must be transformed by the renewing of our minds? (v. 2) How is the Christian mindset different from the non-Christian mindset?

- Why does Paul tell us we shouldn't think too highly of ourselves? (v. 3) How would having that attitude affect the way we're supposed to function as a body of believers? (vv. 4-5)

- How does Paul say the gifts are supposed to be used? (v. 6) What is the connection between having faith and using our gifts?

APPLY
Application Qs

- How does being a living sacrifice today compare with the sacrifices the Israelites offered to God in the Old Testament? Do you see any similarities?

- Would you consider yourself a living sacrifice for God? Are there any areas of your life that show you're not a living sacrifice?

- Has your relationship with God influenced (or transformed) the way you live? If so, how? Are there things you do now that you didn't do before? Are there things you *don't* do now that you used to do?

- Look over the list of spiritual gifts in vv. 6-8. Are there any gifts you believe you might have? Have you used any of these gifts?

OPTIONAL ACTIVITY

Have your kids each make a list of all the gifts listed in Romans 12:6-8. Have them circle the gifts they know they have, put a line through the gifts they know they don't have, and a question mark next to the gifts they're not sure if they have. Then have everyone share their gift list with the group, and let the other members help select each member's "top gift." Come up with one action item for each group member so that person can begin using his or her gifts in some way.

QUIET TIME REFLECTIONS

Day 1: Romans 12:1

1. What word or phrase stands out to you from this verse? Why?

2. According to this verse, how do we worship God? Do you usually view worshiping God in the same way?

3. Spend time today worshiping God by being a "living sacrifice."

Day 2: Romans 12:2

1. What word or phrase stands out to you from this verse? Why?

2. What do we need to do in order to live out God's will in our lives? Do you need more help not conforming—or being transformed?

3. Spend time today thinking about the areas of your life that need to be transformed.

Day 3: Romans 12:3

1. What word or phrase stands out to you from this verse? Why?

2. How should we think of ourselves? Why do you suppose Paul says we should do this?

3. Spend time today thinking about areas of your life that need a more "sober judgment." How much has your faith changed you?

Day 4: Romans 12:4-5

1. What word or phrase stands out to you from these verses? Why?

2. According to this passage, is it possible to be a lone-ranger Christian? Why/why not?

3. Spend time today thinking about what it means to belong to the body of Christ.

Day 5: Romans 12:6

1. What word or phrase stands out to you from this verse? Why?

2. Do you suppose Paul says that every Christian has at least one gift? If so, what do you believe yours might be?

3. Spend time today identifying your gift(s) and how you can use your gifting to help others.

Day 6: Romans 12:7-8

1. What word or phrase stands out to you from these verses? Why?

2. What are some of the gifts Paul mentions in these verses? Which one(s) do you believe you might have?

3. Spend time today thanking God for your gift and asking God how you should start using it right now.

Day 7: Romans 12:1-8

Read through the whole passage and write out the verse that spoke to you the most this week. Meditate on that verse today—and for an extra challenge, memorize it!

22. THE MEANING OF LOVE
Romans 12:9-21

OVERVIEW

According to this passage, love isn't something you feel—it's something you do. This is a very different view of love. In our world, love is sung about, written about, and acted out in ways that communicate that it's an overwhelming emotion. When you feel this "love," it compels you to act. But that's completely different from the love Paul describes in this passage.

Paul doesn't say, "Be devoted in romantic love." Paul says, "Be devoted in brotherly love." Paul doesn't use verbs such as *feel, want,* or *desire.* Instead he uses verbs such as *cling, honor,* and *share.* What does this tell you?

According to Paul, we don't feel love and then act; instead we're to act first and then love. The surprising thing is that the more we act, the more we love; and the feelings, if they weren't there in the first place, eventually come. But we're never dependent on those feelings. That way we can be much more consistent in our love.

Your teens will see that this passage describes the kind of love we're to demonstrate toward one another. And it's a reflection of the kind of love God has for us.

SHARE
Warm-Up Qs

- Do you think of love as a feeling or an action? Why?

- How is the love you have for a boyfriend/girlfriend different from the love you have for a parent? Which is stronger? Which has stronger feelings?

- Is there anyone in your life you love even when you don't feel like it? If so, who?

OBSERVE
Observation Qs

- What kind of love does v. 10 say we should have for one another? What does the second half of this verse say about the way we should live out that love?

- What three instructions are given in v. 12? According to v. 13, how are we supposed to treat people in need?

- What do vv. 15-16 say about our relationships with one another? When are we supposed to rejoice? When are we supposed to mourn? How are we supposed to treat people we consider "lower" than us?

- According to v. 19, why aren't we supposed to take revenge? How do vv. 20-21 say we are to overcome evil?

THINK
Interpretation Qs

- How would you define "brotherly love"? (v. 10) Why do you suppose Paul makes this distinction when he discusses love? What's the difference between brotherly love and romantic love?

- What's the difference between what Paul discusses in vv. 11-12, and what he discusses in vv. 13-16? What is his purpose for telling Christians to live this way?

- Look at what Paul says in v. 18. Why do you suppose he adds the phrase "as far as it depends on you"? Why doesn't he just say "live at peace with everyone"?

- Paul quotes Proverbs in v. 20 to describe what happens when we're good to our enemies. What is the result? Based on your experience, do you believe this is true?

APPLY
Application Qs

- Why do you believe God wants us to love through our actions rather than our feelings? Is there a difference?

- Have you ever tried to love an enemy? If so, describe the experience. Is there someone in your life right now who'd be really difficult for you to love?

- Who do you need to show more love to through your actions? What's one thing you could do to begin that kind of love?

- Do you believe it's possible to overcome evil with good? Can you think of a specific example of someone who has done that? What's one way you could try that in your own life this week?

OPTIONAL ACTIVITY

Have your group members each name five people they love. Then have them name five people who love them. Are the same people on both lists? If not, why not? Finally, have them look over the first list and share whether there's a difference in the kind of love they have for the people on their lists. Which (if any) love is more based on feeling? Which (if any) is based on obligation? For whom do they have the strongest love? What do they consider the strongest kind of love?

QUIET TIME REFLECTIONS

Day 1: Romans 12:9-10

1. What word or phrase stands out to you from these verses? Why?

2. What does Paul say about love in these verses? Do you feel as though you honor others above yourself?

3. Spend time today thinking about how you can put the needs of others over your own needs.

Day 2: Romans 12:11-13

1. What word or phrase stands out to you from these verses? Why?

2. Of all these statements, which is most challenging for you? Which do you do best?

3. Spend time today thinking about how you can live out your relationship with God in your relationship with others.

Day 3: Romans 12:14-16

1. What word or phrase stands out to you from these verses? Why?

2. Which of these statements is hardest for you? Do you think it's possible to bless those who persecute you? If so, what would that look like?

3. Spend time today thinking about how you can be a better friend to those who love you—and to those who don't love you.

Day 4: Romans 12:17-18

1. What word or phrase stands out to you from these verses? Why?

2. What do you think Paul means when he says "as far as it depends on you, live at peace with everyone"?

3. Spend time today thinking about doing your part to bring peace in all your relationships.

Day 5: Romans 12:19

1. What word or phrase stands out to you from this verse? Why?

2. Why should we not take revenge? Is this hard for you? Why/why not?

3. Spend time today thinking about how to leave your feelings of revenge in the hands of God.

Day 6: Romans 12:20-21

1. What word or phrase stands out to you from these verses? Why?

2. Why do you suppose that treating our enemies with love is like heaping burning coals on their heads? What's Paul's strategy for overcoming evil?

3. Spend time today thinking about how you can overcome evil with good.

Day 7: Romans 12:9-21

Read through the whole passage and write out the verse that spoke to you the most this week. Meditate on that verse today—and for an extra challenge, memorize it!

23. RESPECT FOR AUTHORITY
Romans 13:1-7

OVERVIEW

Have you ever driven onto a military base with a Marine officer? When other Marines see the sticker on your car, they salute you. This can be very cool when you're not a Marine. You get to be saluted just because you're in the car.

The bottom line is, Marines know how to respect authority. And Paul says in this passage that Christians should do the same. Your teens will learn that if people are in authority above them (parents, teachers, or government officials), they're called to respect them because of their position. In doing so, they're respecting the sovereignty of God.

So, we're always called to respect authority. But what people do with their authority will determine whether we respect them as people. When people abuse authority, it's harder to figure out how to respect them. Nevertheless, Paul says that we're called to respect their position of authority in our lives.

This is where the example of the Marines can help. At some point, you may have to respect a position of authority, even if you have trouble with the person in it. It's a little like saluting a car when someone inside the car doesn't necessarily deserve it.

SHARE
Warm-Up Qs

- Who in your life do you consider an authority figure? How do you treat that person (or people)?

- Do you believe we should always respect those in authority over us? Can you think of an example when we shouldn't do that?

- When is it hard for you to respect authority? When is it easy?

OBSERVE
Observation Qs

- Look at v. 1. What phrase does Paul repeat for emphasis? What does he say we're to do?

- According to v. 2, what does rebelling against authority have to do with God? What does Paul say is the result?

- According to v. 4, what is a ruler supposed to be? And if this is true, how does v. 5 say we are to treat rulers?

- What does v. 7 say about giving? According to this verse, how do we know what we're supposed to give those in authority?

THINK
Interpretation Qs

- Look at v. 1. Do you have any problem with what Paul says here? Do you believe God ever allows corrupt people to be in authority? If so, are we still supposed to submit to them?

- What do you suppose Paul is saying in v. 2? If we rebel against authority, are we always rebelling against God? Why/why not?

- If v. 4 describes rulers as God's servants, what do we do with rulers who aren't God's servants? Do we still respect their authority? Is there a way to respect the position without necessarily respecting the person in the position? If so, how?

- What principle does Paul offer in v. 7 regarding how we're to show respect to authority? According to this verse, if someone is a government authority, should that person have authority over every part of our lives? Why/why not?

APPLY
Application Qs

- Who in your life do you really respect? Why do you respect that person? What qualities do you admire most in that person?

- Do you have trouble respecting authority figures in your life? (Hint: Think of the way you treat teachers, parents, coaches, etc.) Does this passage reinforce what you're already doing, or show you something you should be doing differently?

- Is there someone in a position of authority you have a particularly difficult time respecting? What makes it difficult? Do you believe it would help or hurt you to show more respect to that person?

- Is there a difference between gaining respect through authority and gaining authority through respect? If there is a difference, describe it. How can you gain authority through gaining respect?

OPTIONAL ACTIVITY

Make a list (or if you feel like being creative, cut out photos) of some of the authority figures in your kids' lives (e.g., parents, teachers, coaches, principals, pastors, police officers, governor, president). Have them rank in order who has the most authority in their lives, and who has the least. Then have them rank who they respect, the most down to the least. Have your teens share why they ranked them in the order they did, and if there was any connection between how much authority someone has, and how much respect they felt for that person.

QUIET TIME REFLECTIONS

Day 1: Romans 13:1

1. What word or phrase stands out to you from this verse? Why?

2. According to this verse, who established our authorities? Is there an authority in your life you have trouble respecting?

3. Spend time today thinking about how your respect for authority is showing respect to God.

Day 2: Romans 13:2

1. What word or phrase stands out to you from this verse? Why?

2. What happens when we rebel against the authority God has placed in our lives?

3. Spend time today thinking about how to rebel less and obey more.

Day 3: Romans 13:3

1. What word or phrase stands out to you from this verse? Why?

2. According to this verse, how do we free ourselves from having problems with those in authority? Do you find it easy to obey those in authority over you? Why/why not?

3. Spend time today thinking about how to live at peace with those in authority over you.

Day 4: Romans 13:4-5

1. What word or phrase stands out to you from these verses? Why?

From *Studies on the Go: Romans* by Laurie Polich. Permission to reproduce this page granted only for use in buyer's youth group. Copyright © 2010 by Youth Specialties. www.youthspecialties.com

2. Why do you believe Paul encourages us to obey those in authority? Why is this good for us to do as a society? Is it ever *not* good?

3. Spend time today thinking about why those in authority need respect for their positions over us. Who are some authority figures in your life?

Day 5: Romans 13:6

1. What word or phrase stands out to you from this verse? Why?

2. According to Paul, why do we pay taxes? Why do you suppose taxes are important to society?

3. Spend time today thinking about doing your part to help society. What does that look like right now in your life?

Day 6: Romans 13:7

1. What word or phrase stands out to you from this verse? Why?

2. What principle does Paul give in this verse? How does this verse help you know how to respond to those in authority in your life?

3. Spend time today thinking about how you can give those in authority the respect they deserve—depending on their roles in your life.

Day 7: Romans 13:1-7

Read through the whole passage and write out the verse that spoke to you the most this week. Meditate on that verse today—and for an extra challenge, memorize it!

24. DRESSING THE PART
Romans 13:8-14

OVERVIEW

One of the best parts about being in a play is your first dress rehearsal. Somehow, when you put on that costume, you feel so much more like the character you're portraying. There's something about dressing the part that transforms you. That's exactly the point Paul is trying to make in this passage.

When he writes, "Clothe yourself with the Lord Jesus Christ" (v. 14), Paul is telling us to *dress* the part so that we can *live* the part. And Paul tells us what clothes we need in this passage. As Christians, we're the representatives of Christ. If we take the time to clothe ourselves with Jesus' presence, we'll be more likely to live like him in this world.

So...how do we "dress like Jesus"? It's more of an inward costume change than an outward one. In a play you have to remove your own clothes to put on the clothes of your character. As Christians we have to do the same thing—but in an internal, spiritual way.

In this session your teens will learn what that entails.

SHARE
Warm-Up Qs

- What was your favorite Halloween costume growing up? Why was it your favorite?

- When you put on a costume, does it affect the way you behave? If so, how?

- If you had to "dress up" as a Christian, what would you look like?

OBSERVE
Observation Qs

- According to v. 8, what's the only debt we're supposed to have? What's fulfilled when we do this?

- Which commandments are listed in v. 9? How are the commandments summed up at the end of the verse?

- What does Paul say we should put aside in v. 12? What are we supposed to put on?

- According to v. 14, how are we supposed to clothe ourselves? What is the last thing Paul tells us to do in this chapter?

THINK
Interpretation Qs

- Verses 8-9 say that all the commandments are summed up in one commandment. Does following that one compel you to keep all the other commandments? If so, how?

- In v. 12 Paul tells us to "put aside the deeds of darkness and put on the armor of light." What do you suppose that means? What are some of the deeds of darkness? What does it look like to put on the armor of light?

- Why does v. 13 say we should behave at night as we do in the daytime? Do you believe we tend to behave differently when it's light as opposed to when it's dark? If so, why?

- What do you suppose Paul means when he says we should "clothe ourselves" with Christ? (v. 14) Are there some things we can do to look more like Jesus? If so, what?

APPLY
Application Qs

- One of the ways people can see we're Christians is through our love for one another. Is there a difficult person in your life who God may be calling you to love? If so, can Christ's love help you do that?

- What are some things you need to "take off" in order to clothe yourself with Christ? (Hint: Think about any attitudes or sins that stand in your way.)

- What are some things you need to "put on" in order to clothe yourself with Christ? (Hint: Think about any actions or attitudes you need to develop.)

- Do you believe people would identify you as a Christ-follower by the way you act? If not, what needs to change in your life so they will?

OPTIONAL ACTIVITY

Gather some Christian T-shirts, buttons, bracelets, necklaces, visors, or any other related items you can find. Put them in a pile in the middle of the room. Tell your group members that they can each choose one to three items to "dress up" as a Christian. Have them share whether or not they've ever worn any of these items to identify themselves as Christians. Do they think "dressing up" as a Christian is an effective witness? Why/why not? Does it ever help their behavior to identify themselves in this way?

QUIET TIME REFLECTIONS

Day 1: Romans 13:8

1. What word or phrase stands out to you from this verse? Why?

2. What happens to the Law when we love one another? Is there anyone in your life who's hard for you to love?

3. Spend time today praying for someone who's hard for you to love.

Day 2: Romans 13:9

1. What word or phrase stands out to you from this verse? Why?

2. What one rule sums up all the commandments? How does following that rule help you follow the rest?

3. Spend time today thinking about how to love your neighbor as yourself.

Day 3: Romans 13:10

1. What word or phrase stands out to you from this verse? Why?

2. What's Paul's explanation for how loving others fulfills the Law?

3. Spend time today thinking about how one positive commandment fulfills all the negative commandments.

Day 4: Romans 13:11-12

1. What word or phrase stands out to you from these verses? Why?

2. What are we supposed to put aside? How would you define "deeds of darkness"?

3. Spend time today thinking about the deeds of darkness you struggle with, and what it means to put on the armor of light.

Day 5: Romans 13:13

1. What word or phrase stands out to you from this verse? Why?

2. Why do you think Paul advises us to behave like we would in the daytime? How is nighttime different from daytime in regard to the temptations we face?

3. Spend time today thinking about what it means to stay in the light.

Day 6: Romans 13:14

1. What word or phrase stands out to you from this verse? Why?

2. What clothing should we put on for protection? What are some ways to do that?

3. Spend time today thinking about what it means to clothe yourself with Jesus. Is there an action you need to take? A behavior you need to stop?

Day 7: Romans 13:8-14

Read through the whole passage and write out the verse that spoke to you the most this week. Meditate on that verse today—and for an extra challenge, memorize it!

From *Studies on the Go: Romans* by Laurie Polich. Permission to reproduce this page granted only for use in buyer's youth group. Copyright © 2010 by Youth Specialties. www.youthspecialties.com

25. FREEDOM TO CHOOSE
Romans 14:1-12

OVERVIEW

If you've ever attended a multidenominational event, you've seen that different Christians have different ways of expressing their common faith. Some quietly close their eyes and pray. Others lift their hands and shout. Some Christians love to dance. Others don't believe dancing is appropriate. There are also lifestyle differences. Some Christians believe it's okay to have a glass of wine. Others stay away from alcohol in any form. Bottom line: None of these expressions of belief is right or wrong—they're just preferences.

In this passage, your teens will learn the difference between precepts and preferences. Precepts are God's commands, and all of us are supposed to obey God's commands (e.g., avoiding lust and drunkenness); preferences are choices we're permitted within those commands (e.g., whether or not to dance or have a glass of wine). What Paul is saying in this passage is that we need to respect each other's preferences.

Your kids will learn in this session that *different* doesn't necessarily mean *wrong*. The variety of denominations and churches is just a reflection of how big our God really is.

SHARE
Warm-Up Qs

- Do you believe all Christians need to believe the same about everything? Why/why not?

- Can you think of any people who believe in Christ but live out their faith differently than you? If so, what are some of the differences?

- What are some things that all Christians should have in common? Do you believe that belonging to the same denomination is one of those things? Why/why not?

OBSERVE
Observation Qs

- What does Paul say we should do with someone whose faith is weak? (v. 1) On what matters should we avoid passing judgment?

- What do vv. 2-3 say about people who believe differently about food with regard to their faith? What does v. 4 say about why we shouldn't judge others?

- What do vv. 5-6 say people's motivation should be for what they do? According to vv. 7-8, are we on our own regarding our decision making? Who is with us?

- According to vv. 10-12, who is our judge? What do these verses say about the judgment everyone will face?

THINK
Interpretation Qs

- According to vv. 1-3, how should we treat those who believe differently about certain things? Are we supposed to accept people no matter what they do? Why/why not?

- What do vv. 3-4 say about God's grace? Does God support us no matter what we do? Why/why not?

- Verse 5 offers a compelling reason to think through decisions about the way we live. Why do our actions—as Christ-followers—matter? (See vv. 6-7.) In what way do they impact God?

- Who is easier to judge—others or ourselves? Why? For what reason should we not judge others and focus more on ourselves? (See v. 10.)

APPLY
Application Qs

- Have you been friends with a Christian who held different convictions from yours? How did those differences make you feel?

- How can you tell the difference between a personal conviction and a command from God? In what ways can knowing the difference help you when it comes to living your faith?

- What's something you've judged other Christians about that—after reading this passage—you wouldn't judge them for now? Do you believe we should ever judge others? Why/why not?

- Is there anything you're doing that you question in terms of whether or not it's okay with God? If so, what/who can help you decide? How does this passage help you (if at all)?

OPTIONAL ACTIVITY

Convictions and Commands: Have your group members make a list of everything they can think of that's wrong to do as a Christian. Then have them go through the list individually and decide whether or not they believe each "wrong" thing is a conviction or a command (they should circle the commands and put a check next to the convictions). Then as a group they should go through all the convictions they each checked and have them decide if they're personal convictions for them and why.

QUIET TIME REFLECTIONS

Day 1: Romans 14:1

1. What word or phrase stands out to you from this verse? Why?

2. According to this verse, what are we not supposed to do? Why do you think Paul mentions this?

3. Spend time today thinking about the differences you have with other Christ-followers, and whether or not you judge them or accept them.

Day 2: Romans 14:2-3

1. What word or phrase stands out to you from these verses? Why?

2. How does Paul use food to point out the principle of acceptance? Are there other areas like this in which Christians disagree regarding lifestyle and behavior? If so, what?

3. Spend time today thinking about those you know who live out their faith differently than you. Can you accept them, or do you believe you need to help them change?

Day 3: Romans 14:4

1. What word or phrase stands out to you from this verse? Why?

2. Are we accountable to each other in our choices? Or only to God?

3. Spend time today thinking about how the Lord is able to make you stand.

Day 4: Romans 14:5-6

1. What word or phrase stands out to you from these verses? Why?

2. What is the issue Paul talks about in these verses? What helps us form our own convictions?

3. Spend time today thinking about whether you're fully convinced in your own mind about the convictions you have—or if there's an area God might want to speak to you about.

Day 5: Romans 14:7-8

1. What word or phrase stands out to you from these verses? Why?

2. How do these verses describe what it means to be a Christian? Do you feel as though you live the way Paul describes?

3. Spend time today thinking about how everything you do impacts God (and the way God is seen in the world).

Day 6: Romans 14:9-12

1. What word or phrase stands out to you from these verses? Why?

2. Where should we focus when it comes to judgment—on others or on ourselves? What does v. 12 say?

3. Spend time today thinking about whether you've ever looked down on others because of their actions, and how you can stop judging them.

Day 7: Romans 14:1-12

Read through the whole passage and write out the verse that spoke to you the most this week. Meditate on that verse today—and for an extra challenge, memorize it!

26. SUPPORT WHERE IT COUNTS
Romans 14:13-23

OVERVIEW

Have you ever been with someone who wants to lose weight? This can be slightly challenging if you don't need to lose weight. But it can be especially challenging when that friend decides to blow her diet and get a pizza with you. Do you go along with your friend and get that pizza? Or do you help her (and deny yourself) by suggesting you eat carrots instead?

According to this passage, you should go with the carrots. Paul says we do everything we can to keep from causing our brothers and sisters to stumble. In fact, Paul says if your brother or sister is injured by what you eat, you're no longer acting in love (v. 15). Sometimes this means we need to sacrifice our own freedom for the sake of their well-being.

When your kids learn to do this, they'll—in a small way—be identifying with Jesus' sacrifice on the cross. And from that perspective, skipping pizza doesn't seem that hard at all.

SHARE
Warm-Up Qs

- When was the last time you felt judged for something you did? How did it make you feel?

- Have you ever succeeded in making some kind of change for the better (e.g., losing weight, getting good grades, getting in shape, etc.)? If so, what inspired you to do it?

- Are you more apt to change because someone judged you— or supported you? Why?

OBSERVE
Observation Qs

- What does Paul say not to do in v. 13? What does he say we should do instead?

- In v. 14, how does Paul describe his own convictions about food? How does he say we should act on our convictions? (v. 15)

- What reason does v. 16 give for why we shouldn't always do something we believe is okay for us? According to vv. 17-19, what should be our priority in the kingdom of God (with other believers)?

- What principle does Paul offer in v. 21 for how we should act? What does v. 22 say we should do with our beliefs about lifestyle?

THINK
Interpretation Qs

- Look at v. 13. What does it mean to put a "stumbling block" in your brother's way? What are some ways we cause each other to stumble as Christians?

- Paul talks about our freedom and responsibility in vv. 14-18. According to these verses, what's the most important thing? Why do you suppose this is?

- Look at what Paul says about food in vv. 19-21. Can you think of anything besides food that might apply here?

- According to vv. 22-23, how can we tell what's right and wrong? Is this always a personal decision? Or are some things wrong for everyone?

APPLY
Application Qs

- Have you ever supported a friend by making a sacrifice (i.e., not doing something you wanted to do so that your friend would ultimately benefit)? If so, describe the experience.

- Has someone ever made a sacrifice to support you? If so, how did that person's sacrifice make you feel?

- Do you have freedom right now in your relationship with God to do what you want? Is there something you need to avoid right now in order to stay close to God?

- Are there people you know who're struggling with things they need to avoid? If so, how can you show support to them right now?

OPTIONAL ACTIVITY

Have two people from your group stand up—one will represent Temptation, and the other will be a Christian. Have them face each other with Temptation putting his hands on Christian's shoulders. Have someone else stand behind Christian and support her by putting hands on Christian's shoulders. Have Temptation press against Christian's shoulders. Then have a second person stand behind Christian, and have Temptation press again. Keep adding people behind Christian, so the more people support, the less Temptation is able to push. Draw analogies to how we can support each other in the body of Christ.

QUIET TIME REFLECTIONS

Day 1: Romans 14:13

1. What word or phrase stands out to you from this verse? Why?

2. What does Paul suggest instead of judging in this verse? What do you think this means for you in your life?

3. Spend time today thinking about ways you can avoid causing others to stumble.

Day 2: Romans 14:14-15

1. What word or phrase stands out to you from these verses? Why?

2. What principle should guide us in our behavior with others? Have others ever told you that something you do makes them feel uncomfortable?

3. Spend time today thinking about how you can support others in their relationships with God.

Day 3: Romans 14:16-18

1. What word or phrase stands out to you from these verses? Why?

2. What's most important in the kingdom of God? Does anything in your life stand in the way of your witness in this way?

3. Spend time today thinking about what's important to God in the way you live your life.

Day 4: Romans 14:19

1. What word or phrase stands out to you from this verse? Why?

2. Where should our effort be as Christians? Are you a peacemaker in your relationships? Is your life an example for others?

3. Spend time today thinking about how you can be a peacemaker in your relationships with others.

Day 5: Romans 14:20-21

1. What word or phrase stands out to you from these verses? Why?

2. When is it wrong to eat or drink something? Have you ever refrained from eating or drinking certain things for the sake of someone else?

3. Spend time today thinking about ways you can support and encourage other Christians through your actions.

Day 6: Romans 14:22-23

1. What word or phrase stands out to you from these verses? Why?

2. Have you ever questioned if something you were doing was okay with God? How does God speak to us about these things?

3. Spend time today asking God if you should refrain from any of your behaviors—for your sake and others' sakes.

Day 7: Romans 14:13-23

Read through the whole passage and write out the verse that spoke to you the most this week. Meditate on that verse today—and for an extra challenge, memorize it!

27. ALL FOR ONE AND ONE FOR ALL
Romans 15:1-13

OVERVIEW

Years ago, a movie was released called *The Mighty*, a story of two friends who come together and form an unlikely bond. One boy, named "Freak," is brilliant but disabled; the other boy, named "Max," is big but slow. At the 4th of July fireworks, Freak can't see above the crowd, so Max puts him on his shoulders. From that moment on, they're never apart.

With Freak as the brains, and Max as the brawn, they draw from each other's strengths and compensate for each other's weaknesses. Paul says it's similar for us in the body of Christ. We're strong in some areas and weak in others. So we're supposed to use our strengths to help others in their weakness, and draw from others' strengths to help us in our weakness. This is what brings unity to the body of Christ.

Your teens will learn in this session that we can be alone and weak—or together and mighty. The choice is up to us.

SHARE
Warm-Up Qs

- Do you believe it's necessary to agree with people in order to have unity with them? Why/why not?

- Where have you experienced a feeling of unity with others? Was it a group of friends? A sports team? A club? A shared experience? What about your experience made you feel unified?

- What's the best example of unity among Christians you've seen? What's the worst example?

OBSERVE
Observation Qs

- According to vv. 1-2, what's our job as brothers and sisters in Christ? What should our motivation be? How was Christ an example to us? (v. 3)

- According to v. 5, what gives us unity? What does v. 6 say we're supposed to do together as Christ-followers?

- What does v. 7 say brings praise to God? What two groups are mentioned in vv. 8-9 that have been brought together in Christ?

- What gives us joy and peace according to v. 13? What empowers us to overflow with hope?

THINK
Interpretation Qs

- What do you suppose it means to be considered strong in Christ? (v. 1) What do you believe it means to be weak?

- Verse 4 mentions the Scriptures as a source of help for us. In what ways can following the Bible help us grow in our faith?

- What do you suppose Paul means when he writes in v. 7, "Accept one another"? Why does this bring God praise?

- Why do you suppose Paul quotes four Old Testament passages in his discussion of the Gentiles? (vv. 9-12) As you think about his audience, what would be Paul's purpose in using the Old Testament so much?

APPLY
Application Qs

- What's the best experience you've had being together with other Christians? What made it so great?

- Has it ever been difficult for you to be unified with other Christians? If so, how did you handle it?

- In what areas would you consider yourself strong as a Christian? In what areas would you consider yourself weak?

- Is there a person in your life who is a stronger Christian than you—and from whom you could learn? Is there a person who's a newer Christian who could learn from you?

OPTIONAL ACTIVITY

(You'll need at least seven people for this—the more, the better!) Have two group members lock arms and two other group members try to pull them apart. Continue adding people to the group with locked arms, and have your two students keep trying to pull them apart. Theoretically this should get harder as the group gets bigger, and will provide a nice object lesson for this study.

QUIET TIME REFLECTIONS

Day 1: Romans 15:1-2

1. What word or phrase stands out to you from these verses? Why?

2. Who do you think Paul is referring to when he speaks of the strong and the weak? Which category do you put yourself in?

3. Spend time today thinking about how you can be stronger in your faith.

Day 2: Romans 15:3-4

1. What word or phrase stands out to you from these verses? Why?

2. What's one thing Paul talks about in these verses that can strengthen your faith? How much do you read the Bible to grow in your faith?

3. Spend time today making a commitment to read your Bible daily so you can grow in your knowledge and understanding of the faith.

Day 3: Romans 15:5-6

1. What word or phrase stands out to you from these verses? Why?

2. What kind of spirit does God give us when we follow Christ? Do you see this among Christians? Why/why not?

3. Spend time today thinking of ways you can be more unified with your brothers and sisters in Christ.

From *Studies on the Go: Romans* by Laurie Polich. Permission to reproduce this page granted only for use in buyer's youth group. Copyright © 2010 by Youth Specialties.
www.youthspecialties.com

Day 4: Romans 15:7-9

1. What word or phrase stands out to you from these verses? Why?

2. How are we supposed to follow Christ's example according to these verses? What does that mean in your life?

3. Spend time today thinking of people who are hard for you to accept, and ask God for strength to help you do it.

Day 5: Romans 15:10-12

1. What word or phrase stands out to you from these verses? Why?

2. Why do you suppose Paul points out verses that include Gentiles with the Jews? How is Paul bringing unity to all believers with what he writes here?

3. Spend time today praying for unity among believers—in all churches and all nations.

Day 6: Romans 15:13

1. What word or phrase stands out to you from this verse? Why?

2. What does Paul say we'll have if we trust in God? Do you find that you have more joy and peace when you're trusting in God?

3. Spend time today thinking about areas of your life in which you need to trust God more so you can experience God's peace.

Day 7: Romans 15:1-13

Read through the whole passage and write out the verse that spoke to you the most this week. Meditate on that verse today—and for an extra challenge, memorize it!

28. GOD'S PURPOSE FOR YOUR LIFE
Romans 15:14-33

OVERVIEW

Frederick Buechner once wrote that your purpose in life is where your greatest passion meets the world's greatest need. Paul illustrates that as he describes his calling in this chapter.

Paul's greatest passion was to share Christ with others. The world's greatest need was where Christ had not yet been preached. So this passage describes how Paul became a missionary by matching his passion with the world's need.

How blessed we are that Paul followed God's call! How blessed others will be if we do the same! When I get to the end of my life, God won't ask, "Laurie, why weren't you Moses?" But how sad it would be if God asked, "Laurie, why weren't you Laurie?"

In this session your teens will be encouraged to explore what God's purpose might be for them. And they still have their whole lives ahead of them to live it out.

SHARE
Warm-Up Qs

- If someone asked you, "What's your purpose in life?" how would you respond?

- Can you think of someone who's fulfilling his or her purpose? Who? What about him/her makes you feel that way?

- Can you sense when God is leading you to do something? If so, how?

OBSERVE
Observation Qs

- How does Paul describe himself in v. 16? Who is he a minister to? What is his duty?

- What was Paul's ambition according to v. 20? What does v. 19 say about how Paul fulfilled that ambition? What does v. 22 say about what he hasn't been able to do because of this?

- According to vv. 23-24, what is Paul longing for? What does he plan to do on the way to Spain? What does he want the Romans to do with him?

- What does Paul know about his visit to the Romans according to v. 29? What does he ask them to do in vv. 30-32?

THINK
Interpretation Qs

- As you read vv. 15-16, do you believe Paul is clear about his purpose in life? How would you describe his purpose? How do you suppose Paul received direction for this?

- Would you describe Paul as single-minded, based on v. 18? If so, why? Do you believe this helped Paul fulfill God's purpose for him?

- What did Paul have a passion for, according to vv. 20-21? How does v. 22 prove that Paul prioritized his passion?

- As you read vv. 23-28, what do you sense about the way Paul was led in his life? How do you believe he decided where to go and what to do? How does v. 29 answer this question?

APPLY

Application Qs

- Have you ever had a sense that God was leading you in your life? If so, describe the circumstance.

- Is there anything you feel passionate about in your life? (In other words, something you're good at, something you enjoy, etc.) If so, are you doing anything about it right now?

- Someone once said that your calling is where your greatest passion meets the world's greatest need. Can you think of how your passion could be used to meet a need?

- Do you have a sense of God's purpose in your life? If so, what is it? If not, what can you do to open yourself to hear what that purpose might be? (e.g., seek a spiritual mentor, get involved in a Bible study, ask for prayer support, etc.)

OPTIONAL ACTIVITY

Write Your Epitaph: Have your kids write down the words they'd like to have on their tombstones. How would they like to be remembered? What would they like to have accomplished? What impact would they want to have on the world? After they're through, have them write down what they need to do to become the person they described on their "tombstones."

QUIET TIME REFLECTIONS

Day 1: Romans 15:14-16

1. What word or phrase stands out to you from these verses? Why?

2. What's Paul's purpose for instructing the believers? Who is instructing you in the faith so you can instruct others? Are you instructing anyone now?

3. Spend time today thinking about someone with less Bible knowledge than you, and ask God how you can come alongside that person to help him or her grow in faith.

Day 2: Romans 15:17-19

1. What word or phrase stands out to you from these verses? Why?

2. Who does Paul glory in? Do you glory more in God or yourself?

3. Spend time today thinking of ways to give God the glory for your accomplishments.

Day 3: Romans 15:20-22

1. What word or phrase stands out to you from these verses? Why?

2. What is Paul's ambition? Do you have the same ambition with friends and family members who don't know Christ?

3. Spend time today praying for someone you know who doesn't know Christ—and ask God to open a door for you to share the gospel with that person.

Day 4: Romans 15:23-24

1. What word or phrase stands out to you from these verses? Why?

2. How do you view Paul's level of affection for the people he is writing to?

3. Spend time today thanking God for friends you haven't seen in a while.

Day 5: Romans 15:25-29

1. What word or phrase stands out to you from these verses? Why?

2. What drives Paul to move from place to place? What's his main mission?

3. Spend time today thinking about whether or not sharing your faith is a priority in your life.

Day 6: Romans 15:30-33

1. What word or phrase stands out to you from these verses? Why?

2. What does Paul ask for in these verses? How do you see the closeness he shares with other believers?

3. Spend time today thinking about your Christian support— and thank God for how that support strengthens you.

Day 7: Romans 15:14-33

Read through the whole passage and write out the verse that spoke to you the most this week. Meditate on that verse today—and for an extra challenge, memorize it!

29. FRIENDS IN CHRIST
Romans 16:1-16

OVERVIEW

What do you appreciate about your friends? When was the last time you told them? In this passage Paul illustrates the importance not only of having friends, but also of affirming and encouraging them. And reading his words will inspire you to do the same.

The words people say to us can be powerful in their influence. Think about some of the words that have been spoken to you. For good or for bad, people take in and respond to the words that are spoken to them. And encouraging words can make the difference in determining what we become. That's why this passage is so important.

The words Paul uses to affirm his friends show the importance of being generous with our affirmation and specific in our appreciation. In this session your teens will have the opportunity to follow his example.

SHARE
Warm-Up Qs

- What are the top-three qualities you appreciate in a good friend?

- Do you believe it's important that your closest friends share the same faith as you? Why/why not?

- When was the last time someone encouraged you with something they said (i.e., words of affirmation or affection)? What was said to you?

OBSERVE
Observation Qs

- Who does Paul talk about at the beginning of his greeting? (vv. 1-2) How does he describe her? What does Paul ask the Christians in Rome to do for her?

- What do we learn about Priscilla and Aquila in vv. 3-5? What group is included in their greeting? (v. 5)

- How did Andronicus and Junias express their friendship to Paul? (v. 7) What does Paul say about the timing of when they came to Christ?

- How many women does Paul affirm in vv. 1-16? How many men? What are some of the things Paul commends them for?

THINK
Interpretation Qs

- Given the culture Paul was in, do you believe it's significant that he begins his greeting with an affirmation of a woman? Why/why not?

- As you look over the whole list of Paul's greetings (vv. 1-16), what are some things he appreciates in other Christians?

Can you tell what Paul values in friendship by the things he says? If so, what are they?

- What do you learn about women in the early church from vv. 4, 6, 7, 12, and 15? Do you believe it was controversial for Paul to refer to some of the women as apostles (v. 7), saints (v. 15), and coleaders of the church (v. 5)? Why/why not?

- What do we learn about Paul's relationships with his friends from these greetings? Do you imagine he considered his friends as if they were family? What does v. 16 indicate regarding the kinds of relationships Paul wants his friends to have with each other?

APPLY
Application Qs

- Do you believe it's important to appreciate your friends? If so, what are some ways you can do that? Who is someone you can appreciate this week?

- Do you have friends who have encouraged you in your relationship with God? If so, who? If not, is there anyone you know who could be that kind of friend?

- Would you say you're a bigger influence on your friends—or are they a bigger influence on you? Why?

- Do you feel content with your friendships right now? Or do you need to find some new friends? How do you think God feels about your friendships?

OPTIONAL ACTIVITY

Time of Affirmation: Take turns letting every person in your group get affirmed by the others in the group. (If it's a big group, you may want to limit the number of affirmations per person to three.) Encourage your teens to be specific in their affirmations—naming the qualities they see, and the reasons they appreciate them. You can also have group members write their affirmations so each group member can keep them (and remember what was said).

QUIET TIME REFLECTIONS

Day 1: Romans 16:1-2

1. What word or phrase stands out to you from these verses? Why?

2. What does Paul say about Phoebe in these verses? Do you believe you would be described as a "servant of the church" by those you know?

3. Spend time today thinking of ways you can serve in your church.

Day 2: Romans 16:3-5

1. What word or phrase stands out to you from these verses? Why?

2. What did Priscilla and Aquila do for Paul? Do you have that kind of relationship with any of your friends?

3. Spend time today thanking God for friends who have your back.

Day 3: Romans 16:6-8

1. What word or phrase stands out to you from these verses? Why?

2. Who in these verses came to the faith before Paul? Who in your life has been a Christian longer than you?

3. Spend time today thanking God for friends and family who knew Christ before you did—and for what they can teach you about living the Christian faith.

From *Studies on the Go: Romans* by Laurie Polich. Permission to reproduce this page granted only for use in buyer's youth group. Copyright © 2010 by Youth Specialties. www.youthspecialties.com

Day 4: Romans 16:9-11

1. What word or phrase stands out to you from these verses? Why?

2. What does Paul say about Apelles in v. 10? Do you believe other Christians could describe you in this way?

3. Spend time today thinking of ways your faith has been tested, and whether or not you have stood strong.

Day 5: Romans 16:12-13

1. What word or phrase stands out to you from these verses? Why?

2. How does Paul commend women in these verses? Do you have someone (besides your mom) who's been like a mother to you?

3. Spend time today thanking God for the mothers and fathers placed in our lives who're outside of our families.

Day 6: Romans 16:14-16

1. What word or phrase stands out to you from these verses? Why?

2. What does Paul call his friends in v. 15? Do you feel as though you're a saint? Why/why not?

3. Spend time today thanking God for being the one who makes you a saint.

Day 7: Romans 16:1-16

Read through the whole passage and write out the verse that spoke to you the most this week. Meditate on that verse today—and for an extra challenge, memorize it!

30. FINAL WORDS
Romans 16:17-27

OVERVIEW

Now Paul is ready to sign off. But he has some final words to say before he's through. The first thing he says is to be wise about the company you keep. This is good advice. Whether you like it or not, you are influenced by the people around you.

Your kids may notice that when they become friends with other kids, they often start talking like them, acting like them, and having the same mannerisms. For that reason, they can get into trouble when they pick the wrong friends!

The other piece of advice Paul gives is to be wise about what's good, and innocent about what's evil. This can be challenging when you live in a culture that does the exact opposite. It's challenging to do the right thing when surrounded by people doing the wrong thing. But we must hold to what we know is true.

In the end, truth will win out. Paul says we can count on it.

SHARE
Warm-Up Qs

- When you write a letter or an email to a friend, how do you usually end it?

- If you had to come up with one sentence that summed up your philosophy of life, what would it be?

- If you knew this was the last time you could communicate with your friends, what would you tell them?

OBSERVE
Observation Qs

- In v. 17, who does Paul tell the Roman Christians to watch out for? What does Paul tell them to do?

- According to v. 19, what does Paul want us to be wise about? What does he want us to be innocent about?

- What does Paul say will happen in v. 20? In the second part of this verse, what does he wish for them in the meantime?

- Who does Paul address his final words to in v. 27? According to vv. 25-26, what does Paul believe God is able to do?

THINK
Interpretation Qs

- Why does Paul warn the Christians in Rome to stay away from the people described in v. 17? Why doesn't he just tell them to be an example to them?

- What do you suppose it means to be "wise about what is good, and innocent about what is evil"? (v. 19) How would you define *good*? How would you define *evil*?

- How do you interpret the promise Paul gives in v. 20? When do you suppose this will happen?

- Look at what Paul says about his writings in vv. 25-26. Do you believe God inspired the writing of his letters? If so, what was God's purpose in that inspiration? Do you believe Paul's letters were written to influence more people than the audience Paul was writing to?

APPLY
Application Qs

- Is there anyone in your life who's a bad influence for your Christian walk? Without naming names, what makes that person a bad influence?

- Which do you need to be—wiser or more innocent? Why?

- If you could give someone one piece of advice for keeping their faith strong, what would it be?

- In what way do you see God establishing you for his kingdom? How have you seen God change you? Is there any area in which you're still changing? What do you believe God still wants to do in you before taking you home?

OPTIONAL ACTIVITY

Have your kids imagine they were chosen as valedictorians, and they each had to give a speech to their graduating class. Ask them what three things they'd want to say to their friends in their speeches about what's important in life.

QUIET TIME REFLECTIONS

Day 1: Romans 16:17-18

1. What word or phrase stands out to you from these verses? Why?

2. What warning does Paul give in this passage? Is there anyone you need to keep your distance from because of the way he or she influences you?

3. Spend time today asking God for wisdom in choosing your relationships.

Day 2: Romans 16:19

1. What word or phrase stands out to you from this verse? Why?

2. What do you believe it means to be wise about what's good and innocent about what's evil? What things do you need to be wise and innocent about?

3. Spend time today asking for discernment regarding your daily choices—and for God's guidance regarding what you choose.

Day 3: Romans 16:20

1. What word or phrase stands out to you from this verse? Why?

2. What is God ultimately going to do with all evil? How does this encourage you today?

3. Spend time today thanking God for being ultimately more powerful than any evil in the world.

Day 4: Romans 16:21-22

1. What word or phrase stands out to you from these verses? Why?

2. Who wrote down the letter of Romans for Paul? How is this person's greeting from Paul different than the others?

3. Spend time today thanking God for people who help you in your work—at school and at home.

Day 5: Romans 16:23-24

1. What word or phrase stands out to you from these verses? Why?

2. What does Paul say about Gaius? Do you know people with the gift of hospitality who open their homes to you?

3. Spend time today thanking God for people who are hospitable in your life.

Day 6: Romans 16:25-27

1. What word or phrase stands out to you from these verses? Why?

2. What's Paul's final word to the Romans? Who does Paul give glory to?

3. Spend time today giving glory to God for everything in your life.

Day 7: Romans 16:17-27

Read through the whole passage and write out the verse that spoke to you the most this week. Meditate on that verse today—and for an extra challenge, memorize it!

Studies on the Go: John is a quick, pick-up-and-use Bible study that doesn't skimp on depth. You won't need to rewrite quetions or reconfigure anything because author (and small group guru) Laurie Polich has made sure every question is appropriate for students. The 30 studies inside will engage your group with open-ended questions and practical applications from the spiritual wisdom of John's Gospel.

Studies on the Go: John

Laurie Polich
Retail $9.99
978-0-310-27200-7

Visit www.youthspecialties.com
or your local bookstore.